Data Science
Essentials

T0282054

by Lillian Pierson, PE

for
dummies®
A Wiley Brand

Data Science Essentials For Dummies®

Published by: **John Wiley & Sons, Inc.**, 111 River Street, Hoboken, NJ 07030-5774, www.wiley.com

For general information on our other products and services, please contact our Customer Care Department within the U.S. at 877-762-2974, outside the U.S. at 317-572-3993, or fax 317-572-4002. For technical support, please visit https://hub.wiley.com/community/support/dummies.

Wiley publishes in a variety of print and electronic formats and by print-on-demand. Some material included with standard print versions of this book may not be included in e-books or in print-on-demand. If this book refers to media such as a CD or DVD that is not included in the version you purchased, you may download this material at http://booksupport.wiley.com. For more information about Wiley products, visit www.wiley.com.

Library of Congress Control Number: 2024949382

ISBN 978-1-394-29700-9 (pbk); ISBN 978-1-394-29702-3 (ebk); ISBN 978-1-394-29701-6 (ebk)

SKY10090207_110624

Table of Contents

Introduction

This book was written as much for expert data scientists as it was for aspiring ones. Its content represents a new approach to doing data science — one that puts business vision and profitably at the heart of our work as data scientists.

Data science and artificial intelligence (AI) have disrupted the business world so radically that it's nearly unrecognizable compared to what things were like just 10 or 15 years ago. The good news is that most of these changes have made everyone's lives and businesses more efficient, more fun, and dramatically more interesting. The bad news is that if you don't yet have at least a modicum of data science competence, your business and employment prospects are growing dimmer by the moment.

Since 2014, when this book was first written (throughout the first several editions), I've harped on this same point. Lots of people listened! So much has changed about data science over the years, however, that this book has needed two full rewrites since it was originally published. What changed? The math and scientific approach that underlie data science haven't changed one bit. But over the years, with all the expansion of AI adoption across business and with the remarkable increase in the supply of data science workers, the data science landscape has seen a hundredfold increase in diversity with respect to what people and businesses are using data science to achieve.

The original idea behind this book when it was first published was to provide "a reference manual to guide you through the vast and expansive areas encompassed by data science." At the time, not too much information out there covered the breadth of data science in one resource. That's changed!

Data scientist as a title only really began to emerge in 2012. Most of us practitioners in the field back then were all new and still finding our way. In 2014, I didn't have the perspective or confidence I needed to write a book like the one you're reading now. Thank you so much to all the readers who have read this book previously, shared positive feedback, and applied what they learned to create better lives for themselves and better outcomes for their companies. The positive transformation of my readers is a big part of what keeps me digging deep to produce the very best version of this book that I possibly can.

The internet is full of *information for the sake of information* — information that lacks the depth, context, and relevance that are needed to transform that information to true meaning in the lives of its consumers. Publishing more of this type of content doesn't help people — it confuses them, overwhelms them, and wastes their precious time! When writing this book for a third time, I took a radical stance against "information for the sake of information."

I also want to make three further promises about the content in this book: It's meaningful, it's actionable, and it's relevant. If it isn't one of these three adjectives, I've made sure it hasn't made its way into this book.

In this book, I detail what data science actually is and what its theoretical underpinnings are. You'll find references to ancillary materials that directly support what you're learning within these pages. All these support materials are hosted on the companion website for this book: https://businessgrowth.ai. I highly recommend you take advantage of those assets — I've donated many of them from my archived bank of limited-edition paid products.

Note: If you want me to show you how to implement the data science that's discussed in this book, I have two Python for Data Science Essential Training courses on LinkedIn Learning. You're most welcome to follow up by taking those courses. You can access them both directly through my course author page on LinkedIn Learning: www.linkedin.com/learning/instructors/lillian-pierson-p-e.

About This Book

In keeping with the *For Dummies* brand, this book is organized in a modular, easy-to-access format that allows you to use the book as an owner's manual. The book's chapters are structured to walk you through a clear process, so reading them in order may make the most sense. You don't absolutely *have* to read the book from cover to cover, however — you can glean a great deal from jumping around, although now and then you may miss some important context by doing so.

Within this book, you may note that some web addresses break across two lines of text. If you're reading this book in print and want to visit one of these web pages, simply key in the web address exactly as it's noted in the text, pretending as though the line break doesn't exist. If you're reading this as an e-book, you've got it easy — just click the web address to be taken directly to the web page.

Foolish Assumptions

In writing this book, I've assumed that you're comfortable with advanced tasks in Microsoft Excel — pivot tables, grouping, sorting, plotting, and the like. Having strong skills in algebra, basic statistics, or even business calculus helps as well. Foolish or not, it's my high hope that all readers have subject matter expertise to which they can apply the skills presented in this book. Because data scientists need to know the implications and applications of the data insights they derive, subject matter expertise is a major requirement for data science.

Icons Used in This Book

As you make your way through this book, you see the following icons in the margins:

TIP

The Tip icon marks tips (duh!) and shortcuts you can use to make subject mastery easier.

REMEMBER

The Remember icon marks information that's especially important to know. To siphon off the most important information in each chapter, just skim the material next to these icons.

WARNING

The Warning icon tells you to watch out! It marks important information that may save you headaches.

Where to Go from Here

If you're new to data science, you're best off starting from Chapter 1 and reading the book from beginning to end. If you already know the data science basics, I suggest that you read the last part of Chapter 1, skim Chapter 2, and then dig deep into the rest of the book.

This book is unlike any other data science book or course on the market. How do I know? Because I created it from scratch based on my own unique experience and perspective. That perspective is based on nearly 20 years of consulting experience within the data, technology, and engineering domains. This book is not a remake of what some other expert wrote in *their* book — it's an original work of art and a labor of love for me. If you enjoy the contents of this book, please reach out to me at lillian@data-mania.com and let me know.

Helping readers like you is my mission in life!

Chapter **1**

Wrapping Your Head Around Data Science

For over a decade now, *everyone* has been absolutely deluged by data. It's coming from every computer, every mobile device, every camera, and every imaginable sensor — and now it's even coming from watches and other wearable technologies. Data is generated in every social media interaction we humans make, every file we save, every picture we take, and every query we submit; data is even generated when we do something as simple as ask a favorite search engine for directions to the closest ice cream shop.

If you're anything like I was, you may have wondered, "What's the point of all this data? Why use valuable resources to generate and collect it?" Although even just two decades ago, no one was in a position to make much use of most of the data that's generated, the tides today have definitely turned. Specialists known as *data engineers* are constantly finding innovative and powerful new ways to capture, collate, and condense unimaginably massive volumes of data. Other specialists known as *data scientists* are leading change by deriving valuable and actionable insights from that data.

In its truest form, data science represents the optimization of processes and resources. Data science produces *data insights* — actionable, data-informed conclusions or predictions that you can use to understand and improve your business, your investments, your health, and even your lifestyle and social life. Using data science insights is like being able to see in the dark. For any goal or pursuit you can imagine, you can find data science methods to help you predict the most direct route from where you are to where you want to be — and to anticipate every pothole in the road between both places.

In this chapter, I explain the difference between data science and data engineering.

Seeing Who Can Make Use of Data Science

The terms *data science* and *data engineering* are often misused and confused, so let me start off by clarifying that these two fields are, in fact, separate and distinct domains of expertise. *Data science is the computational science of extracting meaningful insights from raw data and then effectively communicating those insights to generate value. Data engineering,* on the other hand, is an engineering domain that's dedicated to building and maintaining systems that overcome data processing bottlenecks and data handling problems for applications that consume, process, and store large volumes, varieties, and velocities of data.

In both data science and data engineering, you commonly work with the following types of data:

>> **Structured data:** Data that is stored, processed, and manipulated in a traditional *relational database management system* (RDBMS). An example of this type of data can be seen in the tabular schema of rows and columns you'd commonly encounter when working with corporate databases.

>> **Unstructured data:** Data that is commonly generated from human activities and doesn't fit into a structured database format. Examples of unstructured data are data that comprises email documents, Microsoft Word documents or audio or video files.

>> **Semistructured data:** Data that doesn't fit into a structured database system but is nonetheless organizable by tags that are useful for creating a form of order and hierarchy in the data. XML and JSON files are examples of data that comes in semistructured form.

In the past, only large tech companies with massive funding had the skills and computing resources required to implement data science methodologies to optimize and improve their business, but that hasn't been the case for quite a while now. The proliferation of data has created a demand for insights, and this demand is embedded in many aspects of modern culture — from the Uber passenger who expects the driver to show up exactly at the time and location predicted by the Uber app to the online shopper who expects the Amazon platform to recommend the best product alternatives for comparing similar goods before making a purchase. Data and the need for data-informed insights are ubiquitous. Because organizations of all sizes are beginning to recognize that they're immersed in a sink-or-swim, data-driven, competitive environment, data know-how has emerged as a core and requisite function in almost every line of business.

What does this mean for the average knowledge worker? It means that everyday employees are increasingly expected to support a progressively advancing set of technological and data requirements. Why? Because almost all industries are reliant on data technologies and the insights they spur. Consequently, many people are in continuous need of upgrading their data skills, or else they face the real possibility of being replaced by a more data-savvy employee.

The good news is that upgrading data skills doesn't usually require people to go back to college or earn a university degree in statistics, computer science, or data science. The bad news is that, even with professional training or self-teaching, it always takes extra work to stay industry-relevant and tech-savvy. In this respect, the data revolution isn't so different from any other change that has hit industry in the past. The fact is, in order to stay relevant, you need to take the time and effort to acquire the skills that keep you current. When you're learning how to do data science, you can take some courses, educate yourself using online resources, read books like this one, and attend events where you can learn what you need to know to stay on top of the game.

Who can use data science? You can. Your organization can. Your employer can. Anyone who has a bit of understanding and training can begin using data insights to improve their lives, their careers, and the well-being of their businesses. Data science represents a change in the way you approach the world. When determining outcomes, people once used to make their best guess, act on that guess, and then hope for the desired result. With data insights, however, people now have access to the predictive vision that they need to truly drive change and achieve the results they want.

Here are some examples of ways you can use data insights to make the world, and your company, a better place:

>> **Develop key performance indicators (KPIs) for your business systems.** Use KPIs to track performance and optimize the return on investment (ROI) for measurable business activities.

>> **Develop your marketing strategy.** Use data insights and predictive analytics to identify marketing strategies that work, eliminate underperforming efforts, and test new marketing strategies.

>> **Keep communities safe.** Predictive policing applications help law enforcement personnel predict and prevent local criminal activities.

>> **Help make the world a better place for those less fortunate.** Data scientists in developing nations are using social data, mobile data, and data from websites to generate real-time analytics that improve the effectiveness of humanitarian responses to disasters, epidemics, food scarcity issues, and more.

Inspecting the Pieces of the Data Science Puzzle

To practice data science, in the true meaning of the term, you need the analytical know-how of math and statistics, the coding skills necessary to work with data, and an area of subject matter expertise. Without this expertise, you may as well call yourself a mathematician or a statistician. Similarly, a programmer without subject matter expertise and analytical know-how may better be considered a software engineer or developer, but not a data scientist.

The need for data-informed business and product strategy has been increasing exponentially for about a decade now, forcing all business sectors and industries to adopt a data science approach. As such, different flavors of data science have emerged. The following are just a few titles under which experts of every discipline are required to know and regularly do data science:

» Clinical biostatistician

» Data and tech policy analyst

» Data scientist–geospatial and agriculture analyst

» Data scientist–health care

» Digital banking product owner

» Director of data science–advertising technology

» Geotechnical data scientist

» Global channel ops–data excellence lead

Nowadays, it's almost impossible to differentiate between a proper data scientist and a subject matter expert (SME) whose success depends heavily on their ability to use data science to generate insights. Looking at a person's job title may or may not be helpful, simply because many roles are titled *data scientist* when they may as well be labeled data strategist or product manager, based on the actual requirements. In addition, many knowledge workers are doing daily data science and not working under the title of *data scientist*. It's an overhyped, often misleading label that's not always helpful if you're trying to find out what a data scientist does by looking at online job boards.

To shed some light, in the following sections I spell out the key components that are part of any data science role, regardless of whether that role is assigned the *data scientist* label.

Collecting, querying, and consuming data

Data engineers have the job of capturing and collating large volumes of structured, unstructured, and semistructured *big data* (an outdated term that's used to describe data that exceeds the processing capacity of conventional database systems because it's too big, it moves too fast, or it lacks the structural requirements of traditional database architectures).

REMEMBER

Data engineering tasks are separate from the work that's performed in data science, which focuses more on analysis, prediction, and visualization. Despite this distinction, whenever data scientists collect, query, and consume data during the analysis process, they perform work similar to that of the data engineer (the role I tell you about earlier in this chapter).

Although valuable insights can be generated from a single data source, often the combination of several relevant sources delivers the contextual information required to drive better data-informed decisions. A data scientist can work from several datasets that are stored in a single database, or even in several different data storage environments. At other times, source data is stored and processed on a cloud-based platform built by software and data engineers.

No matter how the data is combined or where it's stored, if you're a data scientist, you almost always have to *query* data — in other words, write commands to extract relevant datasets from data storage systems. Most of the time, you use Structured Query Language (SQL) to query data. (Chapter 7 is all about SQL, so if the acronym scares you, jump ahead to that chapter now.)

Whether you're using a third-party application or doing custom analyses by using a programming language such as R or Python, you can choose from a number of universally accepted file formats:

>> **Comma-separated values (CSV):** Almost every brand of desktop and web-based analysis application accepts this file type, as do commonly used scripting languages such as Python and R.

>> **Script:** Most data scientists know how to use Python to analyze and visualize data. These script files end with the extension .ply or .ipynb (Python).

>> **Application:** Excel is useful for quick-and-easy, spot-check analyses on small- to medium-size datasets. These application files have the .xls or .xlsx extension.

>> **Web programming:** If you're building custom, web-based data visualizations, you may be working in D3.js — or data-driven documents, a JavaScript library for data visualization. When you work in D3.js, you use data to manipulate web-based documents using `.html`, `.svg`, and `.css` files.

Applying mathematical modeling to data science tasks

Data science relies heavily on a practitioner's math skills (and statistics skills, as described in the following section) precisely because these are the skills needed to understand your data and its significance. These skills are also valuable in data science because you can use them to carry out predictive forecasting, decision modeling, and hypotheses testing.

REMEMBER

Mathematics uses deterministic methods to form a *quantitative* (or *numerical*) description of the world; *statistics* is a form of science that's derived from mathematics, but it focuses on using a *stochastic* (probabilities) approach and inferential methods to form a quantitative description of the world. (I tell you more about math and statistics in Chapter 4.) Data scientists use mathematical methods to build decision models, generate approximations, and make predictions about the future. Chapter 4 presents many mathematical approaches that are useful when working in data science.

REMEMBER

In this book, I assume that you have a fairly solid skill set in basic math — you'll benefit if you've taken college-level calculus or even linear algebra. I try hard, however, to meet you where you are. I realize that you may be working based on a limited mathematical knowledge (advanced algebra or maybe business calculus), so I convey advanced mathematical concepts using a plain-language approach that's easy for everyone to understand.

Deriving insights from statistical methods

In data science, statistical methods are useful for better understanding your data's significance, for validating hypotheses, for simulating scenarios, and for making predictive forecasts of future events. Advanced statistical skills are somewhat rare, even among quantitative analysts, engineers, and scientists. If you want to go places in data science, though, take some time to get up to speed in a few basic statistical methods, like linear and logistic regression, Naïve Bayes classification, and time series analysis. (These methods are covered in Chapter 4.)

Coding, coding, coding — it's just part of the game

Coding is unavoidable when you're working in data science. You need to be able to write code so that you can instruct the computer on how to manipulate, analyze, and visualize your data. Programming languages like Python are important for writing scripts for data manipulation, analysis, and visualization. SQL, on the other hand, is useful for data querying.

Although coding is a requirement for data science, it doesn't have to be this big, scary *thing* that people make it out to be. Your coding can be as fancy and complex as you want it to be, but you can also take a rather simple approach. Although these skills are paramount to success, you can pretty easily learn enough coding to practice high-level data science. I've dedicated Chapters 6 and 7 to helping you get to know the basics of what's involved in getting started in Python and querying in SQL, respectively.

Applying data science to a subject area

Statisticians once exhibited some measure of obstinacy in accepting the significance of data science. Many statisticians have cried out, "Data science is nothing new — it's just another name for what we've been doing all along!" Although I can sympathize with their perspective, I'm forced to stand with the camp of data scientists who markedly declare that data science is separate, and definitely distinct, from the statistical approaches that comprise it.

My position on the unique nature of data science is based to some extent on the fact that data scientists often use computer languages not used in traditional statistics and take approaches derived from the field of mathematics. But the main point of distinction between statistics and data science is the need for subject matter expertise.

Because statisticians usually have only a limited amount of expertise in fields outside of statistics, they're almost always forced to consult with an SME to verify exactly what their findings mean and to determine the best direction in which to proceed. Data scientists, on the other hand, should have a strong subject matter expertise in the area in which they're working. Data scientists generate deep insights and then use their domain-specific expertise to understand exactly what those insights mean with respect to the area in which they're working.

Here are a few ways in which today's knowledge workers are coupling data science skills with their respective areas of expertise in order to amplify the results they generate:

>> **Clinical informatics scientists** combine their health-care expertise with data science skills to produce personalized health-care treatment plans. They use health-care informatics to predict and preempt future health problems in at-risk patients.

>> **Marketing data scientists** combine data science with marketing expertise to predict and preempt customer *churn* (the loss of customers from a product or service to that of a competitor's). They also optimize marketing strategies, build recommendation engines, and fine-tune marketing mix models.

>> **Data journalists** *scrape* websites (extract data in bulk directly from the pages on a website) for fresh data in order to discover and report the latest breaking-news stories. (I talk more about data storytelling in Chapter 8.)

>> **Directors of data science** bolster their technical project management capabilities with an added expertise in data science. Their work includes leading data projects and working to protect the profitability of the data projects for which they're responsible. They also act to ensure transparent communication between C-suite executives, business managers, and the data personnel on their team who actually do the implementation work.

>> **Data product managers** supercharge their product management capabilities with the power of data science. They use data science to generate predictive insights that better inform decision-making around product design, development, launch, and strategy.

>> **Machine learning engineers** combine software engineering superpowers with data science skills to build predictive applications. This is a classic data implementation role, more of which I discuss in Chapter 2.

Communicating data insights

As a data scientist, you must have sharp verbal communication skills. If a data scientist can't communicate, all the knowledge and insight in the world does *nothing* for the organization. Data scientists need to be able to explain data insights in a way that staff members can understand. Not only that, but data scientists need to be able to produce clear and meaningful data visualizations and written narratives. Most of the time, people need to see a concept for themselves in order to truly understand it. Data scientists must be creative and pragmatic in their means and methods of communication. (I cover the topics of data visualization and data-driven storytelling in much greater detail in Chapter 8.)

IN THIS CHAPTER

» Unraveling the data story

» Looking at important data sources

» Differentiating data science from data engineering

» Storing data on-premises or in a cloud

» Exploring other data engineering solutions

Chapter **2**

Tapping into Critical Aspects of Data Engineering

Though data and artificial intelligence (AI) are extremely interesting topics in the eyes of the public, most laypeople aren't aware of what data really is or how it's used to improve people's lives.

This chapter tells the full story of modern data ecosystems; explains where data comes from and how it's used; and outlines the roles that machine learning engineers, data engineers, and data scientists play. In this chapter, I introduce the fundamental concepts related to storing and processing data for data science so this information can serve as the basis for laying out your plans for leveraging data science to improve business performance.

Defining the Three Vs

If companies want to stay competitive, they must be proficient and adept at infusing data insights into their processes and products, as well as their growth and management strategies. This is especially true in light of the digital adoption explosion that occurred as a direct result of the COVID-19 pandemic. Whether your data volumes rank on the terabyte or petabyte scales, data-engineered solutions must be designed to meet requirements for the data's intended destination and use.

Three characteristics — also called "the three Vs" — are the key identifiers by which you can understand your data: volume, velocity, and variety. Because the three Vs of data are continually expanding, newer, more innovative technologies must continuously be developed to manage these problems.

Grappling with data volume

In its raw form, most data is *low value* — in other words, the value-to-data-quantity ratio is low in raw data. Much data is composed of huge numbers of very small transactions that come in a variety of formats. These incremental components produce true value only after they're aggregated and analyzed. Roughly speaking, data engineers have the job of aggregating data, and data scientists have the job of analyzing it.

Handling data velocity

Most data is created by using automated processes and instrumentation nowadays, and because data storage costs are relatively inexpensive, system velocity is, many times, the limiting factor. Keep in mind that raw data is low value. Consequently, you need systems that are able to ingest a lot of it, on short order, to generate timely and valuable insights.

In engineering terms, *data velocity* is data volume per unit time. Latency is a characteristic of all data systems, and it quantifies the system's delay in moving data after it has been instructed to do so. Many data-engineered systems are required to have latency less than 100 milliseconds, measured from the time the data is created to the time the system responds.

Throughput is a characteristic that describes a system's capacity for work per unit time. Throughput requirements can easily be as high as 1,000 messages per second in data systems! High-velocity, real-time moving data presents an obstacle to timely decision-making. The capabilities of data-handling and data-processing technologies often limit data velocities.

Tools that intake data into a system — otherwise known as data ingestion tools — come in a variety of flavors.

Dealing with data variety

The data explanation gets even more complicated when you add unstructured and semistructured data to structured data sources. This *high-variety* data comes from a multitude of sources. The most salient point about it is that it's composed of a combination of datasets with differing underlying structures (structured, unstructured, or semistructured). Heterogeneous, high-variety data is often composed of any combination of graph data, JSON files, XML files, social media data, structured tabular data, weblog data, and data that's generated from user clicks on a web page — otherwise known as *click-streams*.

Structured data can be stored, processed, and manipulated in a relational database management system (RDBMS) — an example of this type of system would be a PostgreSQL database that uses a tabular schema of rows and columns, making it easier to identify specific values within data that's stored within the database. This data, which can be generated by humans or machines, is derived from all sorts of sources — from click-streams and web-based forms to point-of-sale transactions and sensors. *Unstructured data* comes completely unstructured — it's commonly generated from human activities and doesn't fit into a structured database format; such data can be derived from blog posts, emails, and Microsoft Word documents. *Semistructured data* doesn't fit into a structured database system but is nonetheless structured by tags that are useful for creating a form of order and hierarchy in the data. Semistructured data is commonly found in databases and file systems. It can be stored as log files, XML files, or JSON data files.

Become familiar with the term *data lake.* It's used by practitioners in the industry to refer to a nonhierarchical data storage system that's used to hold huge volumes of multistructured, raw data within a flat storage architecture — in other words, a collection of records that come in uniform format and that are not cross-referenced in any way. You can use the Amazon Simple Storage Service (S3) platform — or a similar cloud storage solution — to meet the same requirements on the cloud. (The Amazon S3 platform is one of the more popular cloud architectures available for storing data.)

WARNING

Although both the terms *data lake* and *data warehouse* are used to refer to storing data, the terms refer to different types of systems. *Data lake* is defined in the preceding paragraph; a *data warehouse* is a centralized data repository that you can use to store and access only structured data. A more traditional data warehouse system commonly employed in business intelligence solutions is a *data mart* — a storage system (for structured data) that you can use to store one particular focus area of data, belonging to only one line of business in the company.

Identifying Important Data Sources

Vast volumes of data are continually generated by humans, machines, and sensors everywhere. Typical sources include data from social media, financial transactions, health records, clickstreams, log files, and the *internet of things* (IoT) — a web of digital connections that joins together the ever-expanding array of devices that consumers use in their everyday lives.

Grasping the Differences among Data Approaches

Data science, machine learning engineering, and data engineering cover different functions within the *data paradigm* — an approach wherein huge velocities, varieties, and volumes of structured, unstructured, and semistructured data are being captured, processed, stored, and analyzed using a set of techniques and technologies that are completely novel compared to those that were used in decades past.

All these functions are useful for deriving knowledge and actionable insights from raw data. All are essential elements for any comprehensive decision-support system, and all are extremely helpful when formulating robust strategies for future business growth. Although the terms *data science* and *data engineering* are often used interchangeably, they're distinct domains of expertise. Over the past five years, the role of machine learning engineer has risen up to bridge a gap that exists between data science and data engineering.

In the following sections, I introduce concepts that are fundamental to data science and data engineering, as well as the hybrid machine learning engineering role. Then I show you how these roles function in an organization's data team.

Defining data science

If *science* is a systematic method by which people study and explain domain-specific phenomena that occur in the natural world, you can think of *data science* as the scientific domain that's dedicated to knowledge discovery via data analysis.

Data scientists use mathematical techniques and algorithmic approaches to derive solutions to complex business and scientific problems. Data science practitioners use its predictive methods to derive insights that are otherwise unattainable. In business and in science, data science methods can provide more robust decision-making capabilities:

>> **In business,** the purpose of data science is to empower businesses and organizations with the data insights they need in order to optimize organizational processes for maximum efficiency and revenue generation.

>> **In science,** data science methods are used to derive results and develop protocols for achieving the specific scientific goal at hand.

Data science is a vast and multidisciplinary field. To call yourself a true data scientist, you need to have expertise in math and statistics, computer programming, and your own domain-specific subject matter.

Using data science skills, you can do cool things like the following:

>> Use *machine learning* (the practice of applying algorithms to learn from — and make automated predictions from — data) to optimize energy usage and lower corporate carbon footprints.

>> Optimize tactical strategies to achieve goals in business and science.

>> Predict for unknown contaminant levels from sparse environmental datasets.

>> Design automated theft- and fraud-prevention systems to detect anomalies and trigger alarms based on algorithmic results.

>> Craft site-recommendation engines for use in land acquisitions and real estate development.

>> Implement and interpret predictive analytics and forecasting techniques for net increases in business value.

Data scientists must have extensive and diverse quantitative expertise to be able to solve these types of problems.

Defining machine learning engineering

A *machine learning engineer* is essentially a software engineer who is skilled enough in data science to deploy advanced data science models within the applications they build, thus bringing machine learning models into production in a live environment like a software as a service (SaaS) product or even just a web page.

Contrary to what you may have guessed, the role of machine learning engineer is a hybrid between a data scientist and a software engineer, *not* a data engineer. A machine learning engineer is, at their core, a well-rounded software engineer who also has a solid foundation in machine learning and AI. This person doesn't need to know as much data science as a data scientist, but they should know much more about computer science and software development than a typical data scientist.

Defining data engineering

If *engineering* is the practice of using science and technology to design and build systems that solve problems, you can think of *data engineering* as the engineering domain that's dedicated to building and maintaining data systems for overcoming data processing bottlenecks and data handling problems that arise from handling the high volume, velocity, and variety of data.

Data engineers use skills in computer science and software engineering to design systems for, and solve problems with, handling and manipulating datasets. Data engineers often have experience working with (and designing) real-time processing frameworks, as well as with RDBMSs. They generally code in Java, C++, Python, or Scala. They know how to deploy Spark to handle, process, and refine raw data into datasets with more manageable sizes. Simply put, with respect to data science, the purpose of data engineering is to engineer large-scale data solutions by building coherent, modular, and scalable data processing platforms from which data scientists can subsequently derive insights.

REMEMBER

Most engineered systems are *built* systems — they're constructed or manufactured in the physical world. Data engineering is different, though. It involves designing, building, and implementing software solutions to problems in the data world — a world that can seem abstract when compared to the physical reality of the Golden Gate Bridge or the Aswan High Dam.

Using data engineering skills, you can, for example:

>> Integrate data pipelines with the natural language processing (NLP) services that were built by data scientists at your company.

>> Build mission-critical data platforms capable of processing more than 10 billion transactions per day.

>> Tear down data silos by finally migrating your company's data from a legacy on-premises data storage environment to a cutting-edge cloud warehouse.

>> Enhance and maintain existing data infrastructure and data pipelines.

Data engineers need solid skills in computer science, database design, and software engineering to be able to perform this type of work.

Comparing machine learning engineers, data scientists, and data engineers

The roles of data scientist, machine learning engineer, and data engineer are frequently conflated by hiring managers. If you look around at most position descriptions for companies that are hiring, they often mismatch the titles and roles or simply expect applicants to be the Swiss Army knife of data skills and be able to do them all.

TIP

If you're hiring someone to help make sense of your data, be sure to define the requirements clearly before writing the position description. Because data scientists must also have subject matter expertise in the particular areas in which they work, this requirement generally precludes data scientists from also having much expertise in data engineering. And, if you hire a data engineer who has data science skills, that person generally won't have much subject matter expertise outside of the data domain. Be prepared to call in a subject matter expert (SME) to help out.

Because many organizations combine and confuse roles in their data projects, data scientists are sometimes stuck having to learn to do the job of a data engineer — and vice versa. To come up with the highest-quality work product in the least amount of time, hire a data engineer to store, migrate, and process your data; a data scientist to make sense of it for you; and a machine learning engineer to bring your machine learning models into production.

REMEMBER

Lastly, keep in mind that data engineer, machine learning engineer, and data scientist are just three small roles within a larger organizational structure. Managers, midlevel employees, and business leaders also play a huge part in the success of any data-driven initiative.

Storing and Processing Data for Data Science

In the following sections, I explain the basics of what's involved in both cloud and on-premises data storage and processing.

Storing data and doing data science directly in the cloud

After you've realized the upside potential of storing data in the cloud, it's hard to look back. Storing data in a cloud environment offers serious business advantages:

>> **Faster time to market (TTM):** Many cloud service providers take care of the bulk of the work that's required to configure, maintain, and provision the computing resources that are required to run jobs within a defined system — also known

as a *compute environment*. This dramatically increases ease of use and ultimately allows for faster TTM for data products.

>> **Enhanced flexibility:** Cloud services are extremely flexible with respect to usage requirements. If you set up in a cloud environment and then your project plan changes, you can simply turn off the cloud service with no further charges incurred. This isn't the case with on-premises storage, because after you purchase the server, you own it. Your only option from then on is to extract the best possible value from a noncancelable resource.

>> **Security:** If you go with reputable cloud service providers — like Amazon Web Services (AWS), Google Cloud, or Microsoft Azure — your data is likely to be a whole lot more secure in the cloud than it would be on-premises. That's because of the sheer number of resources that these megalith players dedicate to protecting and preserving the security of the data they store. I can't think of a multinational company that would have more invested in the security of its data infrastructure than Amazon, Google, or Microsoft.

A lot of different technologies have emerged in the wake of the cloud computing revolution. The next sections examine a few of these new technologies.

Using serverless computing to execute data science

When we talk about serverless computing, the term *serverless* is quite misleading because the computing, indeed, takes place on a server. *Serverless computing* really refers to computing that's executed in a cloud environment rather than on your desktop or on-premises at your company. The physical host server exists, but it's 100 percent supported by the cloud computing provider retained by you or your company.

One great tragedy of modern-day data science is the amount of time data scientists spend on non-mission-critical tasks like data collection, data cleaning and reformatting, data operations, and data integration. By most estimates, only 10 percent of a data scientist's time is spent on predictive model building; the rest of it is spent trying to prepare the data and the data infrastructure for that mission-critical task they've been retained to complete. Serverless computing has been a game changer for the data science industry because it decreases the downtime that data scientists spend in preparing data and infrastructure for their predictive models.

Earlier in this chapter, I talk a bit about SaaS. Serverless computing offers something similar: *function as a service* (FaaS), a containerized cloud computing service that makes it much faster and simpler to execute code and predictive functions directly in a cloud environment, without the need to set up complicated infrastructure around that code. With serverless computing, your data science model runs directly within its container, as a sort of stand-alone function. Your cloud service provider handles all the provisioning and adjustments that need to be made to the infrastructure to support your functions.

Examples of popular serverless computing solutions are AWS Lambda, Google Cloud Run functions, and Azure Functions.

Containerizing predictive applications within Kubernetes

Kubernetes is an open-source software suite that manages, orchestrates, and coordinates the deployment, scaling, and management of containerized applications across clusters of worker nodes. One particularly attractive feature about Kubernetes is that you can run it on data that sits in on-premises clusters, in the cloud, or in a hybrid cloud environment.

The chief focus of Kubernetes is helping software developers build and scale apps quickly. Though it does provide a fault-tolerant, extensible environment for deploying and scaling predictive applications in the cloud, Kubernetes also requires quite a bit of data engineering expertise to set them up correctly.

REMEMBER

A system is fault tolerant if it's built to continue successful operations despite the failure of one or more of its subcomponents. This requires redundancy in computing nodes. A system is described as *extensible* if it's flexible enough to be extended or shrunk in size without disrupting its operations.

To overcome this obstacle, Kubernetes released its Kubeflow product, a machine learning toolkit that makes it simple for data scientists to directly deploy predictive models within Kubernetes containers, without the need for outside data engineering support.

Sizing up popular cloud-warehouse solutions

You have a number of products to choose from when it comes to cloud-warehouse solutions. Here are the most popular options:

» **Amazon Redshift** (https://aws.amazon.com/redshift): A popular data warehousing service that runs atop data sitting within the Amazon cloud, Redshift is most notable for the incredible speed at which it can handle data analytics and business intelligence workloads. Because it runs on the AWS platform, Redshift's fully managed data warehousing service has the incredible capacity to support petabyte-scale cloud storage requirements. If your company is already using other AWS products — like Amazon EMR, Amazon Athena, or Amazon Kinesis — Redshift is the natural choice to integrate nicely with your existing technology. Redshift offers both pay-as-you-go and on-demand pricing structures that you'll want to explore further on its website.

» **Snowflake** (www.snowflake.com): This SaaS solution provides powerful, parallel-processing analytics capabilities for both structured and semistructured data stored in the cloud on Snowflake's servers. Snowflake is the ultimate three-in-one solution, with its cost-effective data storage, analytical processing capabilities, and all the built-in cloud services you may need. Snowflake integrates well with analytics tools like Qlik and Tableau, as well as with technologies like Apache Kafka, Apache Spark, and Pentaho, but it wouldn't make sense if you're already relying mostly on Amazon services. Pricing for Snowflake is based on the amount of data you store, as well as on the execution time for compute resources you consume on the platform.

» **Google BigQuery** (https://cloud.google.com/bigquery): Touted as a serverless data warehouse solution, BigQuery is a relatively cost-effective solution for generating analytics from data sources stored in the Google Cloud. Similar to Snowflake and Redshift, BigQuery provides fully managed cloud services that make it fast and simple for data scientists and analytics professionals to use the tool without the need for assistance from in-house data engineers. Analytics can be generated on petabyte-scale data. BigQuery integrates with Google Data Studio, Looker, Power BI, and Tableau for ease of use when it comes to post-analysis data storytelling. Pricing for BigQuery is based on the amount of data you store, as well as on the compute resources you consume on the platform, as represented by the amount of data your queries return from the platform.

Introducing NoSQL databases

An RDBMS is designed to handle only relational datasets constructed of data that is stored in clean rows and columns and, thus, is capable of being queried via Structured Query Language (SQL). RDBMSs are incapable of handling unstructured and semistructured data. Plus, RDBMSs simply lack the processing and handling capabilities that are needed for meeting data volume and velocity requirements.

This is where *NoSQL* comes in — its databases are nonrelational, distributed database systems that were designed to rise to the challenges involved in storing and processing data. They can be run on-premises or in a cloud environment. NoSQL databases step out past the relational database architecture and offer a much more scalable, efficient solution. NoSQL systems facilitate non-SQL data querying of nonrelational or schema-free, semistructured and unstructured data. In this way, NoSQL databases are able to handle the structured, semistructured, and unstructured data sources that are common in data systems.

NoSQL offers four categories of nonrelational databases: graph databases, document databases, key-values stores, and column family stores. Because NoSQL offers native functionality for each of these separate types of data structures, it offers efficient storage and retrieval functionality for most types of nonrelational data. This adaptability and efficiency makes NoSQL an increasingly popular choice for handling data and for overcoming processing challenges that come along with it.

NoSQL applications like Apache Cassandra and MongoDB are used for data storage and real-time processing. Apache Cassandra is a popular type of key-value store NoSQL database, and MongoDB is the most-popular document-oriented type of NoSQL database. It uses dynamic schemas and stores JSON-esque documents.

Processing data in real-time

A *real-time processing framework* is — as its name implies — a framework that processes data in real time (or near real time) as the data streams and flows into the system. Real-time frameworks process data in microbatches — they return results in a matter of seconds rather than the hours or days it typically takes batch-processing frameworks like MapReduce. Real-time processing frameworks do one of the following:

>> **Increase the overall time efficiency of the system.** Solutions in this category include Apache Flink and Apache Spark for near-real-time stream processing.

>> **Deploy innovative querying methods to facilitate the real-time querying.** Some solutions in this category are Apache Drill, Google's Dremel, Shark for Apache Hive, and Apache Impala.

Apache Spark is an in-memory computing application that you can use to query, explore, analyze, and even run machine learning algorithms on incoming streaming data in near real time. Its power lies in its processing speed: The ability to process and make predictions from streaming data sources in three seconds flat is no laughing matter.

TIP

Real-time, stream-processing frameworks are quite useful in a multitude of industries — from stock and financial market analyses to e-commerce optimizations and from real-time fraud detection to optimized order logistics. Regardless of the industry in which you work, if your business is impacted by real-time data streams that are generated by humans, machines, or sensors, a real-time processing framework would be helpful to you in optimizing and generating value for your organization.

Recognizing the Impact of Generative AI

Now that you've gotten an overview of traditional data storage and processing methods, it's time to explore some of the more cutting-edge ways that AI technologies are reshaping the data engineering landscape.

The reshaping of data engineering

When performed manually, data cleaning, augmentation, and preprocessing tasks consume a substantial amount of time and resources. These tasks are now being accelerated by the use of generative AI (GenAI) models to generate synthetic data that mimics real-world datasets, thereby filling gaps in data or expanding the volume of training data for machine learning models. This capability improves the quality and robustness of AI models while also reducing the manual effort involved in data preparation.

GenAI is also useful for automatically generating code snippets, such as SQL queries and data transformation scripts. This, of course, streamlines the development of data pipelines and reduces errors. By integrating GenAI into their workflows, data engineers are achieving faster, more efficient data processing while significantly fortifying their capacity to deploy machine learning models at scale.

Tools and frameworks for supporting AI workloads

To fully harness the power of GenAI in data engineering, a range of specialized tools and frameworks are available to support AI workloads. Leading the charge are open-source libraries like TensorFlow and PyTorch, which offer robust environments for developing, training, and deploying complex AI models. These frameworks are increasingly being integrated into data engineering pipelines, thereby enabling seamless processing and manipulation of large datasets.

Additionally, frameworks like Hugging Face Transformers provide pretrained models and tools that simplify the deployment of GenAI in various applications, including NLP and data generation. Cloud-based AI services like Amazon SageMaker, Google AI Platform, and Microsoft Azure AI further enhance this ecosystem by offering scalable, managed environments that cater to the demands of training and deploying AI models in real time.

These services provide the computational power needed for intensive AI workloads while also providing integrated tools for data management. This, in turn, makes it easier for data engineers to build and maintain AI-infused data pipelines.

Chapter **3**

Using a Machine to Learn from Data

I f you've been paying attention to the news over the past decade, you've no doubt heard of a concept called *machine learning* — often referenced when reporters are covering stories on the newest amazing invention from artificial intelligence (AI). In this chapter, you dip your toes into the area called machine learning.

Defining Machine Learning and Its Processes

Machine learning is the practice of applying algorithmic models to data over and over again so that your computer discovers hidden patterns or trends that you can use to make predictions. Machine learning has a vast and ever-expanding assortment of use cases, including the following:

» Real-time internet advertising

» Internet marketing personalization

» Internet search

- >> Spam filtering
- >> Recommendation engines
- >> Natural language processing (NLP) and sentiment analysis
- >> Automatic facial recognition
- >> Customer churn prediction
- >> Credit score modeling
- >> Survival analysis for mechanical equipment

Walking through the steps of the machine learning process

Three main steps are involved in machine learning: setup, learning, and application. Setup involves acquiring data, preprocessing it, selecting the most appropriate variables for the task at hand (called *feature selection*), and breaking the data into training and test datasets. You use the *training data* to train the model, and the *test data* to test the accuracy of the model's predictions. The learning step involves model experimentation, training, building, and testing. The application step involves model deployment and prediction.

REMEMBER

Here's a rule of thumb for breaking data into test and training sets: Apply random sampling to two-thirds of the original dataset in order to use that sample to train the model. Use the remaining one-third of the data as test data, for evaluating the model's predictions.

Becoming familiar with machine learning terms

Before diving too deeply into a discussion of machine learning methods, you need to know about the (sometimes confusing) vocabulary associated with the field. Because machine learning is an offshoot of both traditional statistics and computer science, it has adopted terms from both fields and added a few of its own. Here's what you need to know:

- >> **Instance:** The same as a *row* (in a data table), an *observation* (in statistics), and a *data point.* Machine learning practitioners are also known to call an instance a *case.*

>> **Feature:** The same as a *column* or *field* (in a data table) and a *variable* (in statistics). In regression methods, a feature is also called an *independent variable* (IV).

>> **Target variable:** The same as a *predictant* or *dependent* variable (DV) in statistics.

REMEMBER

In machine learning, *feature selection* is a somewhat straightforward process for selecting appropriate variables; for *feature engineering*, you need substantial domain expertise and strong data science skills to manually design input variables from the underlying dataset. You use feature engineering in cases where your model needs a better representation of the problem being solved than is available in the raw dataset.

WARNING

Although machine learning is often referred to in the context of data science and AI, these terms are all separate and distinct. Machine learning is a practice within data science, but there's more to data science than just machine learning. AI often, but not always, involves data science and machine learning. *AI* is a term that describes autonomously acting agents. In some cases, AI agents are robots; in others, they're software applications. If the agent's actions are triggered by outputs from an embedded machine learning model, then the AI is powered by data science and machine learning. On the other hand, if the AI's actions are governed by a rules-based decision mechanism, you can have AI that doesn't actually involve machine learning or data science at all.

Considering Learning Styles

Machine learning can be applied in three main styles: supervised, unsupervised, and semisupervised. Supervised and unsupervised methods are behind most modern machine learning applications, and semisupervised learning is an up-and-coming star.

Learning with supervised algorithms

Supervised learning algorithms require that input data has labeled features. These algorithms learn from known features of that data to produce an output model that successfully predicts labels for new incoming, unlabeled data points. You use supervised learning when you have a labeled dataset composed of historical values that are good predictors of future events. Use cases include survival analysis and fraud detection, among others. Logistic regression is a type of supervised learning algorithm, and you see a little more about it in the "Selecting algorithms based on function" section.

Learning with unsupervised algorithms

Unsupervised learning algorithms accept unlabeled data and attempt to group observations into categories based on underlying similarities in input features, as shown in Figure 3-1. Principal component analysis, k-means clustering, and singular value decomposition are all examples of unsupervised machine learning algorithms. Popular use cases include recommendation engines, facial recognition systems, and customer segmentation.

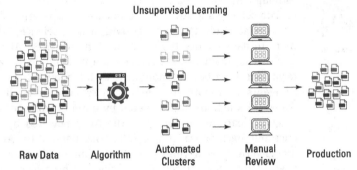

Unsupervised Learning

Raw Data   Algorithm   Automated Clusters   Manual Review   Production

FIGURE 3-1: Unsupervised machine learning breaks down unlabeled data into subgroups.

Learning with reinforcement

Reinforcement learning is a behavior-based learning model. It's based on a mechanic similar to how humans and animals learn. The model is given "rewards" based on how it behaves, and it subsequently learns to maximize the sum of its rewards by adapting the decisions it makes to earn as many rewards as possible.

Seeing What You Can Do

Whether you're just becoming familiar with the algorithms that are involved in machine learning or you're looking to find out more about what's happening in cutting-edge machine learning advancements, this section has something for you. First, I give you an overview of machine learning algorithms, broken down by function; then I describe more about the advanced areas of machine learning that are embodied by deep learning and Apache Spark.

Selecting algorithms based on function

When you need to choose a class of machine learning algorithms, it's helpful to consider each model class based on its functionality:

- **Regression:** You can use this model type to describe and quantify the relationships between independent variables and a dependent variable. This model helps you to identify how changes in the features influence an outcome and it's a very commonly used approach for making predictions. You can read more on linear and logistic regression methods and ordinary least squares in Chapter 4.

- **Association rule learning:** This type of algorithm is a rule-based set of methods that you can use to discover associations between features in a dataset. For an in-depth training and demonstration on how to use association rules in Microsoft Excel, be sure to check out the companion website to this book (`https://businessgrowth.ai`).

- **Instance-based:** If you want to use observations in your dataset to classify new observations based on similarity, you can use this type. To model with instances, you can use methods like k-nearest neighbor classification, covered in Chapter 5.

- **Regularizing:** You can use regularization to introduce added information as a means by which to prevent model overfitting or to solve an ill-posed problem. In case the term is new to you, *model overfitting* is a situation in which a model is so tightly fit to its underlying dataset, as well as its noise or random error, that the model performs poorly as a predictor for new observations.

- **Naïve Bayes:** If you want to predict the likelihood of an event's occurrence based on some evidence in your data, you can use this method, based on classification and regression. Naïve Bayes is covered in Chapter 4.

- **Decision tree:** A tree structure is useful as a decision support tool. You can use it to build models that predict for potential downstream implications that are associated with any given decision.

>> **Clustering:** You can use this type of unsupervised machine learning method to uncover subgroups within an unlabeled dataset. Both k-means clustering and hierarchical clustering are covered in Chapter 5.

>> **Dimension reduction:** If you're looking for a method to use as a filter to remove redundant information, unexplainable random variation, and outliers from your data, consider dimension reduction techniques such as factor analysis and principal component analysis. These topics are covered in Chapter 4.

>> **Neural network:** A neural network mimics how the brain solves problems by using a layer of interconnected neural units as a means by which to learn — and infer rules — from observational data. It's often used in image recognition and computer vision applications.

Imagine that you're deciding whether you should go to the beach. You never go to the beach if it's raining, and you don't like going if it's colder than 75°F outside. These are the two inputs for your decision. Your preference to not go to the beach when it's raining is a lot stronger than your preference to not go to the beach when it's colder than 75°F, so you weight these two inputs accordingly. For any given instance where you decide whether you're going to the beach, you consider these two criteria, add up the results, and then decide whether to go. If you decide to go, your decision threshold has been satisfied. If you decide not to go, your decision threshold was not satisfied. This is a simplistic analogy for how neural networks work.

Now, for a more technical definition. The simplest type of neural network is the *perceptron*. It accepts more than one input, weights them, adds them up on a processor layer, and then — based on the activation function and the threshold you set for it — outputs a result. An *activation function* is a mathematical function that transforms inputs into an output signal. The processor layer is called a *hidden layer*. A *neural network* is a layer of connected perceptrons that all work together as a unit to accept inputs and return outputs that signal whether some criteria is met. A key feature of neural nets is that they're *self-learning* — in other words, they adapt, learn, and optimize per changes in input data. Figure 3-2 is a schematic layout that depicts how a perceptron is structured.

>> **Deep learning method:** This method incorporates traditional neural networks in successive layers to offer deep-layer training for generating predictive outputs. I tell you more about this topic in the next section.

>> **Ensemble algorithm:** You can use ensemble algorithms to combine machine learning approaches to achieve results that are better than would be available from any single machine learning method on its own.

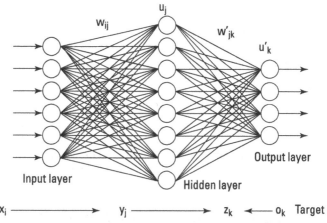

FIGURE 3-2: Neural networks are connected layers of artificial neural units.

TIP

Visit the companion website to this book (https://business growth.ai) to get a quick-start guide to selecting the best deep learning network for your most immediate needs.

If you use Gmail, you must be enjoying its autoreply functionality (the three one-line messages from which you can choose an autoreply to a message someone sent you). This autoreply functionality within Gmail is called Smart Reply, and it's built on deep learning algorithms. Another innovation built on deep learning is Facebook DeepFace, the Facebook feature that automatically recognizes and suggests tags for the people who appear in your Facebook photos. Figure 3-3 is a schematic layout that depicts how a deep learning network is structured.

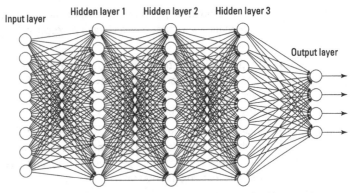

Input layer Hidden layer 1 Hidden layer 2 Hidden layer 3

Output layer

FIGURE 3-3: A deep learning network is a neural network with more than one hidden layer.

Deep learning is a machine learning method that uses hierarchical neural networks to learn from data in an iterative and adaptive manner. It's an ideal approach for learning patterns from unlabeled and unstructured data. It's essentially the same concept as the neural network, except that deep learning algorithms have two or more hidden layers. In fact, computer vision applications — like those that support facial recognition for images uploaded to Facebook, or the self-driving cars produced by Tesla — have been known to implement more than 150 hidden layers in a single deep neural network. The more hidden layers there are, the more complex a decision the algorithm can make.

Generating real-time analytics with Spark

Apache Spark is an in-memory distributed computing application that you can use to deploy machine learning algorithms on large volumes of data that are moving in near real time. From there, generating analytics from these streaming sources is rather straightforward. Whew!

Because it processes data in microbatches, with 3-second cycle times, you can use it to significantly decrease time-to-insight in cases where time is of the essence. It can be run on data that sits in a wide variety of storage architectures, including Amazon Redshift, Amazon Web Services (AWS), Apache Cassandra, Apache Solr, Hadoop Distributed File System (HDFS), and MongoDB. Spark is composed of the following submodules:

>> **Spark SQL:** You use this module to work with and query structured data using Spark. Within Spark, you can query data using Spark's built-in Structured Query Language (SQL) package: SparkSQL. You can also query structured data using Hive, but then you'd use the HiveQL language and run the queries using the Spark processing engine.

>> **GraphX:** The GraphX library is how you store and process network data from within Spark.

>> **Streaming:** The Streaming module is where the data processing takes place. This module basically breaks a continuously streaming data source into much smaller data streams, called *Dstreams* (discreet data streams, in other words). Because the Dstreams are small, these batch cycles can be completed within three seconds, which is why it's called microbatch processing.

>> **MLlib:** The MLlib submodule is where you analyze data, generate statistics, and deploy machine learning algorithms from within the Spark environment. MLlib has application programming interfaces (APIs) for Java, Python, R, and Scala. The MLlib module allows data professionals to work within Spark to build machine learning models in Python or R, and those models will then pull data directly from the requisite data storage repository, whether that be on-premises, in a cloud, or even in a multicloud environment. This helps reduce the reliance that data scientists sometimes have on data engineers. Plus, computations are known to be 100 times faster when processed in-memory using Spark as opposed to the traditional MapReduce framework.

You can deploy Spark on-premises by downloading the open-source framework from the Apache Spark website, at `https://spark.apache.org/downloads.html`. Another option is to run Spark on the cloud via the Apache Databricks service, at `www.databricks.com`.

Chapter **4**

Math, Probability, and Statistical Modeling

M ath and statistics are not the scary monsters that many people make them out to be. In data science, the need for these quantitative methods is simply a fact of life — and nothing to be alarmed about. Although you need to have a handle on the math and statistics that are necessary to solve a problem, you don't need to study for degrees in those fields.

REMEMBER

Contrary to what many pure statisticians would have you believe, the data science field isn't the same as the statistics field. Data scientists have substantive knowledge in one field or several fields, and they use statistics, math, coding, and strong communication skills to help them discover, understand, and communicate data insights that lie within raw datasets related to their field of expertise. Statistics is a vital component of this formula, but not more vital than the others.

In this chapter, I introduce you to the basic ideas behind probability, correlation analysis, dimensionality reduction, decision modeling, regression analysis, outlier detection, and time series analysis.

Exploring Probability and Inferential Statistics

Probability is one of the most fundamental concepts in statistics. To get started making sense of your data by using statistics, you need to be able to identify something as basic as whether you're looking at *descriptive statistics* or *inferential statistics*. You also need a firm grasp of the basics of probability distribution.

A *statistic* is a result that's derived from performing a mathematical operation on numerical data. In general, you use statistics in decision-making. Statistics come in two flavors:

>> **Descriptive:** Descriptive statistics provide a description that illuminates some characteristic of a numerical dataset, including dataset distribution, central tendency (such as mean, min, or max), and dispersion (as in standard deviation and variance). For clarification, the mean of a dataset is the average value of its data points, the min of a dataset is the minimum value of its data points, and the max of a dataset is the maximum value of its data points. Descriptive statistics are not meant to illustrate any causal claims.

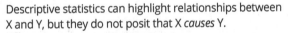

Descriptive statistics can highlight relationships between X and Y, but they do not posit that X *causes* Y.

REMEMBER

>> **Inferential:** Instead of focusing on pertinent descriptions of a dataset, inferential statistics carve out a smaller section of the dataset and try to deduce significant information about the larger dataset. Unlike descriptive statistics, inferential methods, such as regression analysis, *do* try to predict by studying causation. Use inferential statistics to derive information about a real-world measure in which you're interested.

Descriptive statistics describe the characteristics of a numerical dataset, but that doesn't tell you why you should care. In fact, most data scientists are interested in descriptive statistics only because of what they reveal about the real-world measures they describe. For example, a descriptive statistic is often associated with a *degree of accuracy*, indicating the statistic's value as an estimate of the real-world measure.

To better understand this concept, imagine that a business owner wants to estimate the upcoming quarter's profits. The owner may take an average of the past few quarters' profits to use as an estimate of how much profit they'll make during the next quarter. But if the previous quarters' profits varied widely, a descriptive statistic that estimated the *variation* of this predicted profit value (the amount by which this dollar estimate could differ from the actual profits earned) would indicate just how far the predicted value could be from the actual one. (Not bad information to have, right?)

TIP

You can use descriptive statistics in many ways — to detect outliers, for example, or to plan for feature preprocessing requirements or to quickly identify which features you may want (or not want) to use in an analysis.

Like descriptive statistics, *inferential statistics* are used to reveal something about a real-world measure. Inferential statistics do this by providing information about a small data selection, so you can use this information to infer something about the larger dataset from which it was taken. In statistics, this smaller data selection is known as a *sample,* and the larger, complete dataset from which the sample is taken is called the *population.*

If your dataset is too big to analyze in its entirety, pull a smaller sample of this dataset, analyze it, and then make inferences about the entire dataset based on what you learn from analyzing the sample. You can also use inferential statistics in situations where you simply can't afford to collect data for the entire population. In this case, you'd use the data you do have to make inferences about the population at large. At other times, you may find yourself in situations where complete information for the population isn't available. In these cases, you can use inferential statistics to estimate values for the missing data based on what you learn from analyzing the data that's available.

WARNING

For an inference to be valid, you must select your sample carefully so you form a true representation of the population. Even if your sample is representative, the numbers in the sample dataset will always exhibit some *noise* (random variation) indicating that the sample statistic isn't exactly identical to its corresponding population statistic. For example, if you're constructing a sample of data based on the demographic makeup of the population of Chicago, you would want to ensure that proportions of racial/ethnic groups in your sample match up to proportions in the population overall.

Probability distributions

Imagine that you've just rolled into Las Vegas and settled into your favorite roulette table over at the Bellagio. When the roulette wheel spins off, you intuitively understand that there is an equal chance that the ball will fall into any of the slots of the cylinder on the wheel. The slot where the ball lands is totally random, and the *probability* (likelihood) of the ball landing in any one slot over another is the same. Because the ball can land in any slot, with equal probability, there is an equal probability distribution, or a *uniform probability distribution* — the ball has an equal probability of landing in any of the slots in the wheel.

But the slots of the roulette wheel aren't all the same — the wheel has 18 black slots and 20 slots that are either red or green.

$$\text{Probability (black)} = \frac{18}{38} = .4736$$

Because of this arrangement, the probability that your ball will land on a black slot is 47.36 percent.

Your net winnings here can be considered a *random variable*, which is a measure of a trait or value associated with an object, a person, or a place (something in the real world) that is unpredictable. Just because this trait or value is unpredictable, however, doesn't mean that you know nothing about it. What's more, you can use what you *do* know about this thing to help you in your decision-making.

A *weighted average* is an average value of a measure over a very large number of data points. If you take a weighted average of your winnings (your random variable) across the probability distribution, this would yield an *expectation value* — an expected value for your net winnings over a successive number of bets. (An expectation can also be thought of as the best guess, if you had to guess.) To describe it more formally, an *expectation* is a weighted average of some measure associated with a random variable. If your goal is to model an unpredictable variable so that you can make data-informed decisions based on what you know about its probability in a population, you can use random variables and probability distributions to do this.

REMEMBER

When considering the probability of an event, you must know what other events are possible. Always define the set of events as *mutually exclusive* — only one can occur at a time. (Think of the six possible results of rolling a die.) Probability has these two important characteristics:

» The probability of any single event never goes below 0.0 or exceeds 1.0.

» The probability of all events always sums to exactly 1.0.

Probability distribution is classified per these two types:

» **Discrete:** A random variable where values can be counted by groupings

» **Continuous:** A random variable that assigns probabilities to a range of values

REMEMBER

To understand discrete and continuous distribution, think of two variables from a dataset describing cars. A color variable would have a discrete distribution because cars have only a limited range of colors (black, red, or blue, for example). The observations would be countable per the color grouping. A variable describing cars' miles per gallon (mpg) would have a continuous distribution because each car could have its own, separate value for mpg that it gets on average.

» **Normal distributions (numeric continuous):** Represented graphically by a symmetric bell-shaped curve, these distributions model phenomena that tend toward some most-likely observation (at the top of the bell in the bell curve); observations at the two extremes are less likely.

» **Binomial distributions (numeric discrete):** These distributions model the number of successes that can occur in a certain number of attempts when only two outcomes are possible (the old heads-or-tails coin-flip scenario, for example). Binary variables — variables that assume only one of two values — have a binomial distribution.

» **Categorical distributions (non-numeric):** These represent either non-numeric categorical variables or *ordinal variables* (ordered categorical variables). For example, the level of service offered by most airlines is ordinal because they offer first class, business class, and economy class seats.

Conditional probability with Naïve Bayes

You can use the Naïve Bayes machine learning method, which was borrowed straight from the statistics field, to predict the likelihood that an event will occur, given evidence defined in your data features — something called *conditional probability*. Naïve Bayes, which is based on classification and regression, is especially useful if you need to classify text data.

To better illustrate this concept, consider the Spambase dataset that's available from University of California, Irvine's machine learning repository (https://archive.ics.uci.edu/ml/datasets/Spambase). That dataset contains 4,601 records of emails and, in its last field, designates whether each email is spam. From this dataset, you can identify common characteristics between spam emails. After you've defined common features that indicate spam email, you can build a Naïve Bayes classifier that reliably predicts whether an incoming email is spam, based on the empirical evidence supported in its content. In other words, the model predicts whether an email is spam — the *event* — based on features gathered from its content — the *evidence*.

Naïve Bayes comes in these three popular flavors:

>> **MultinomialNB:** Use this version if your variables (categorical or continuous) describe discrete frequency counts, like word counts. This version of Naïve Bayes assumes a multinomial distribution, as is often the case with text data. It doesn't accept negative values.

>> **BernoulliNB:** If your features are binary, you can use multinomial Bernoulli Naïve Bayes to make predictions. This version works for classifying text data but isn't generally known to perform as well as MultinomialNB. If you want to use BernoulliNB to make predictions from continuous variables, that will work, but you first need to subdivide the variables into discrete interval groupings (also known as *binning*).

>> **GaussianNB:** Use this version if all predictive features are normally distributed. It's not a good option for classifying text data, but it can be a good choice if your data contains both positive and negative values (and if your features have a normal distribution, of course).

WARNING

Before building a Bayes classifier naïvely, consider that the model holds an *a priori* assumption — meaning that its predictions are based on an assumption that past conditions still hold true. Predicting future values from historical ones generates incorrect results when present circumstances change.

Quantifying Correlation

Many statistical and machine learning methods assume that your features are independent. To test whether they're independent, though, you need to evaluate their *correlation* (the extent to which variables demonstrate interdependency). In this section, you get a brief introduction to Pearson correlation and Spearman's rank correlation.

TIP

Correlation is quantified per the value of a variable called *r*, which ranges between −1 and 1. The closer the *r*-value is to 1 or −1, the more correlation there is between two variables. If two variables have an *r*-value that's close to 0, it could indicate that they're independent variables.

Calculating correlation with Pearson's *r*

If you wanted to uncover dependent relationships between continuous variables in a dataset, you'd use statistics to estimate their correlation. The simplest form of correlation analysis is the *Pearson correlation*, which assumes the following:

>> Your data is normally distributed.

>> You have continuous, numeric variables.

>> Your variables are linearly related. You can identify a linear relationship by plotting the data points on a chart and looking to see if there is a clear increasing or decreasing trend within the values of the data points, such that a straight line can be drawn to summarize that trend. Figure 4-1 is an illustration of what a linear relationship looks like.

WARNING

Because the Pearson correlation has so many conditions, use it *only* to determine whether a relationship between two variables exists, but not to rule out possible relationships. If you were to get an *r*-value close to 0, it would indicate that there is no linear relationship between the variables but that a nonlinear relationship between them still could exist.

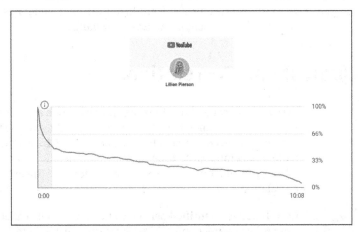

FIGURE 4-1: An example of a linear relationship between months and YouTube subscribers.

To use the Pearson's r to test for linear correlation between two variables, you'd simply plug your data into the following formula and calculate the result:

$$r = \frac{\Sigma(x - \bar{x})(y - \bar{y})}{\sqrt{\Sigma(x - \bar{x})^2 \Sigma(y - \bar{y})^2}}$$

» $\bar{x}$ = mean of x variable

» $\bar{y}$ = mean of y variable

» r = Pearson r coefficient of correlation

After you get a value for your Pearson r, you'd interpret its value according to the following standards:

» **If r is close to +1,** there is a strong positive correlation between the variables.

» **If $r = 0$,** the variables are not linearly correlated.

» **If r is close to –1,** there is a strong negative correlation between the variables.

Ranking variable pairs using Spearman's rank correlation

The Spearman's rank correlation is a popular test for determining correlation between ordinal variables. By applying Spearman's rank correlation, you're converting numeric variable pairs into ranks by calculating the strength of the relationship between variables and then ranking them per their correlation.

The Spearman's rank correlation assumes the following:

>> **Your variables are ordinal.**

>> **Your variables are related nonlinearly.** You can identify nonlinearity between variables by looking at a graph. If the graph between two variables produces a curve (like the one shown in Figure 4-2), then the variables have a nonlinear relationship. This curvature occurs because, with variables related in a nonlinear manner, a change in the value of x doesn't necessarily correspond to the same change in dataset's y-value.

>> **Your data is nonnormally distributed.**

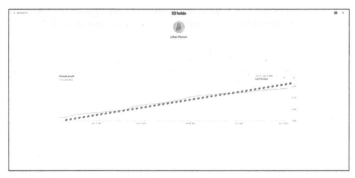

FIGURE 4-2: An example of a nonlinear relationship between watch time and percent viewership.

To use Spearman Rank to test for correlation between ordinal variables, you'd simply plug the values for your variables into the following formula and calculate the result:

$$\rho = 1 - \frac{6\sum d^2}{n(n^2-1)}$$

>> ρ = Spearman's rank correlation coefficient

>> d = difference between the two ranks of each data point

>> n = total number of data points in the dataset

Reducing Data Dimensionality with Linear Algebra

Any intermediate-level data scientist should have a good understanding of linear algebra and how to do math using matrices. Array and matrix objects are the primary data structure in analytical computing. You need them in order to perform mathematical and statistical operations on large and *multidimensional datasets* (datasets with many different features to be tracked simultaneously).

In this section, you see exactly what's involved in using linear algebra and machine learning methods to reduce a dataset's dimensionality — in other words, to reduce a dataset's feature count, without losing the important information the dataset contains, by compressing its features' information into synthetic variables that you can subsequently utilize to make predictions or as input into another machine learning model.

Decomposing data to reduce dimensionality

Okay, what can you do with all this theory? Well, for starters, using a linear algebra method called *singular value decomposition* (SVD), you can reduce the dimensionality of your dataset — in other words, reduce the number of features that you track when carrying out an analysis. Dimension reduction algorithms are ideal if you need to compress your dataset while also removing redundant information and noise. In data science, SVD is applied to analyze principal components from large, noisy, sparse datasets — an approach machine learning folks call *principal component analysis* (PCA). Because the linear algebra involved in PCA is rooted in SVD, let's look at how SVD works.

The SVD linear algebra method decomposes the data matrix into the three resultant matrices shown in Figure 4-4. The product of these matrices, when multiplied together, gives you back your original matrix. SVD is handy when you want to compress or clean your dataset. Using SVD enables you to uncover *latent variables* (inferred variables hidden within your dataset that affect how that dataset behaves). Here are the two main ways to use the SVD algorithm:

>> **Compressing sparse matrices:** If you have a clean yet sparse dataset, you don't want to remove any of the information that the dataset holds, but you do need to compress that information down into a manageable number of variables, so you can use them to make predictions. A handy thing about SVD is that it allows you to set the number of variables, or components, it creates from your original dataset. And if you don't remove any of those components, you'll reduce the size of your dataset without losing any of its important information. This process is illustrated in Figure 4-3.

>> **Cleaning and compressing dirty data:** In other cases, you can use SVD to do an algorithmic cleanse of a dirty, noisy dataset. In this case you'd apply SVD to uncover your components, and then decide which of them to keep by looking at their variance. The industry standard is that explained variance of the components you keep should add up to at least 75 percent or more. This ensures that at least 75 percent of the dataset's original information has been retained within the components you've kept. This process is shown in Figure 4-4.

WARNING

If the sum of the explained variance — or *cumulative variance explained* (CVE) — for the components you keep is less than 95 percent, don't use the components as derived features further downstream in other machine learning models. In this case, the information lost within these derived features will cause the machine learning model to generate inaccurate, unreliable predictions. These derived components are, however, useful as a source for descriptive statistics or for building more general *descriptive analytics* — in other words, analytics that describe what happened in the past, and answer questions like "What happened?," "When?," "How many,?" and "Where?"

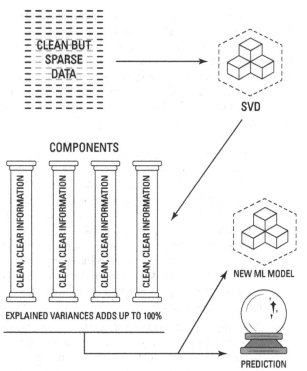

FIGURE 4-3: Applying SVD to compress a sparse, clean dataset.

The lower the CVE, the more you should take your model's results with a grain of salt.

If you remove some components, then when you go to reconstruct your matrix, you'll probably notice that the resulting matrix isn't an exact match to your original dataset. Worry not! That's the data that remains after much of the information redundancy and noise was filtered out by SVD and removed by you.

Getting a little nitty-gritty about SVD, let's look at the formula for SVD, but keep in mind: This is linear algebra not regular algebra, so we're looking at matrix math not regular math. To take it from the beginning, you need to understand the concept of eigenvector. To do that, think of a matrix called *A*. Now consider a nonzero vector called x and that Ax = λx for a scalar λ. In this scenario, scalar λ is what's called an *eigenvalue* of matrix A. It's permitted to take on a value of 0. Furthermore, x is the eigenvector that corresponds to λ, and again, it's not permitted to be a zero value.

λ is simply the scale factor of the eigenvector. SVD decomposes the matrix down into three resultant matrices shown in Figure 4-5. The product of these matrices, when multiplied together, gives you back your original matrix.

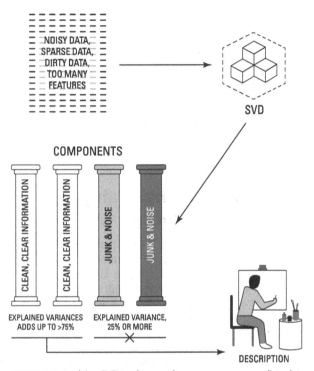

FIGURE 4-4: Applying SVD to clean and compress a sparse, dirty dataset.

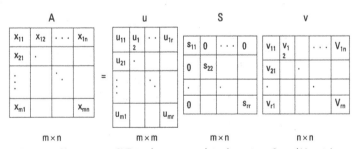

FIGURE 4-5: You can use SVD to decompose data down to u, S, and V matrices.

Take a closer look at Figure 4-5:

$$A = u * S * v$$

>> **A:** This is the matrix that holds all your original data.

>> **u:** This is a left-singular vector (an eigenvector) of A, and it holds all the important, nonredundant information about your data's observations.

>> **v:** This is a right-singular eigenvector of A. It holds all the important, nonredundant information about columns in your dataset's features.

>> **S:** This is the square root of the eigenvalue of A. It contains all the information about the procedures performed during the compression.

Reducing dimensionality with factor analysis

Factor analysis is along the same lines as SVD in that it's a method you can use for filtering out redundant information and noise from your data. An offspring of the psychometrics field, this method was developed to help you derive a root cause in cases where a shared root cause results in *shared variance* — when a variable's variance correlates with the variance of other variables in the dataset.

When you find shared variance in your dataset, that means information redundancy is at play. You can use factor analysis or principal component analysis to clear your data of this information redundancy. You see more on principal component analysis in the following section, but for now, focus on factor analysis and the fact that you can use it to compress your dataset's information into a reduced set of meaningful, non-information-redundant *latent variables* — meaningful inferred variables that underlie a dataset but are not directly observable.

Factor analysis makes the following assumptions:

>> Your features are *metric* (numeric variables on which meaningful calculations can be made).

>> Your features should be continuous or *ordinal*. (If you're not sure what ordinal is, refer back to the first class, business class, and economy class analogy in the "Probability distributions" section of this chapter.)

>> You have more than 100 observations in your dataset and at least 5 observations per feature.

>> Your sample is homogenous.

>> There is $r > 0.3$ correlation between the features in your dataset.

In factor analysis, you do a regression (a topic covered later in this chapter) on features to uncover underlying latent variables, or *factors*. You can then use those factors as variables in future analyses to represent the original dataset from which they're derived. At its core, factor analysis is the process of fitting a model to prepare a dataset for analysis by reducing its dimensionality and information redundancy.

Decreasing dimensionality and removing outliers with PCA

Principal component analysis (PCA) is another dimensionality reduction technique that's closely related to SVD: This unsupervised statistical method finds relationships between features in your dataset and then transforms and reduces them to a set of non-information-redundant *principal components* — uncorrelated features that embody and explain the information that's contained within the dataset (that is, its variance). These components act as a synthetic, refined representation of the dataset, with the information redundancy, noise, and outliers stripped out. You can then use those reduced components as input for your machine learning algorithms to make predictions based on a compressed representation of your data. (For more on outliers, see the "Detecting Outliers" section, later in this chapter.)

The PCA model makes these two assumptions:

>> *Multivariate normality* (MVN) — or a set of real-valued, correlated, random variables that are each clustered around a mean — is desirable, but not required.

>> Variables in the dataset should be continuous.

Although PCA is like factor analysis, they have two major differences: One difference is that PCA does not regress to find some underlying cause of shared variance, but instead decomposes a dataset to succinctly represent its most important information in a reduced number of features. The other key difference is that, with PCA, the first time you run the model, you don't specify the number of components to be discovered in the dataset. You let the initial model results tell you how many components to keep, and then you rerun the analysis to extract those features.

REMEMBER

Similar to the CVE discussion in the SVD part of this chapter, the amount of variance you retain depends on how you're applying PCA, as well as the data you're inputting into the model. Breaking it down based on how you're applying PCA, the following rules of thumb become relevant:

>> **Used for descriptive analytics:** If PCA is being used for descriptive purposes only (for example, when working to build a descriptive avatar of your company's ideal customer), the CVE can be lower than 95 percent. In this case you can get away with a CVE as low as 75 percent to 80 percent.

>> **Used for diagnostic, predictive, or prescriptive analytics:** If principal components are meant for downstream models that generate diagnostic, predictive, or prescriptive analytics, CVE should be 95 percent or higher. Just realize that the lower the CVE, the less reliable your model results will be downstream. Each percentage of CVE that's lost represents a small amount of information from your original dataset that won't be captured by the principal components.

TIP

When using PCA for outlier detection, simply plot the principal components on an x–y scatterplot and visually inspect for areas that may have outliers. Those data points correspond to potential outliers that are worth investigating.

Modeling Decisions with Multiple Criteria Decision-Making

Life is complicated. We're often forced to make decisions where several different criteria come into play, and it often seems unclear which criterion should have priority. Mathematicians, being mathematicians, have come up with quantitative approaches that you can use for decision support whenever you have several criteria or alternatives on which to base your decision. You see those approaches in Chapter 3, where I talk about neural networks and deep learning — another method that fulfills this same decision-support purpose is *multiple criteria decision-making* (MCDM).

Turning to traditional MCDM

You can use MCDM methods in anything from stock portfolio management to fashion-trend evaluation, from disease outbreak control to land development decision-making. Anywhere you have two or more criteria on which you need to base your decision, you can use MCDM methods to help you evaluate alternatives.

To use multiple criteria decision-making, the following two assumptions must be satisfied:

>> **Multiple criteria evaluation:** You must have more than one criterion to optimize.

>> **Zero-sum system:** Optimizing with respect to one criterion must come at the sacrifice of at least one other criterion. This means that there must be trade-offs between criteria — to gain with respect to one means losing with respect to at least one other.

Another important thing to note about MCDM is that it's characterized by binary membership. In mathematics, a *set* is a group of numbers that share a similar characteristic. In traditional set theory, membership is *binary* — in other words, an individual is either a member of a set or it's not. If the individual is a member, it's represented by the number 1, representing a "yes." If it isn't a member, it's represented by the number 0, for "no."

The best way to gain a solid grasp on MCDM is to see how it's used to solve a real-world problem. MCDM is commonly used in investment portfolio theory. Pricing of individual financial instruments typically reflects the level of risk you incur, but an entire portfolio can be a mixture of virtually riskless investments (U.S. government bonds, for example) and minimum-, moderate-, and high-risk investments. Your level of risk aversion dictates the general character of your investment portfolio. Highly risk-averse investors seek safer and less lucrative investments, and less risk-averse investors choose riskier, more lucrative investments. In the process of evaluating the risk of a potential investment, you'd likely consider the following criteria:

>> **Earnings growth potential:** Using a binary variable to score the earnings growth potential, you could say that an investment that falls under a specific earnings growth potential threshold gets scored as 0 (as in "no — the potential is not enough"); anything higher than that threshold gets a 1 (for "yes — the potential is adequate").

>> **Earnings quality rating:** Using a binary variable to score earnings quality ratings, you could say that an investment falling within a particular ratings class for earnings quality gets scored as 1 (for "yes — the rating is adequate"); otherwise, it gets scored as a 0 (as in "no — it's earning quality rating is not good enough").

For you non–Wall Street types out there, *earnings quality* refers to various measures used to determine how kosher a company's reported earnings are; such measures try to answer the question, "Do these reported figures pass the smell test?"

>> **Dividend performance:** Using a binary variable to score dividend performance, you could say that when an invest-ment fails to reach a set dividend performance threshold, it gets a 0 (as in "no — it's dividend performance is not good enough"); if it reaches or surpasses that threshold, it gets a 1 (for "yes — the performance is adequate").

Imagine that you're evaluating 20 different potential invest-ments. In this evaluation, you'd score each criterion for each of the investments. To eliminate poor investment choices, simply sum the criteria scores for each of the alternatives and then dis-miss any investments that don't earn a total score of 3 — leaving you with the investments that fall within a certain threshold of earning growth potential, that have good earnings quality, and whose dividends perform at a level that's acceptable to you.

TIP

For some hands-on practice doing multiple criteria decision-making, go to the companion website to this book (www.business growth.ai) and check out the MCDM practice problem I've left for you there.

Focusing on fuzzy MCDM

If you prefer to evaluate suitability within a range, rather than use binary membership terms of 0 or 1, you can use *fuzzy multiple criteria decision-making* (FMCDM) to do that. With FMCDM you can evaluate all the same types of problems as you would with MCDM. The term *fuzzy* refers to the fact that the criteria being used to evaluate alternatives offer a range of acceptability — instead of the binary, crisp set criteria associated with traditional MCDM. Evaluations based on fuzzy criteria lead to a range of potential outcomes, each with its own level of suitability as a solution.

TIP

One important feature of FMCDM: You're likely to have a list of several fuzzy criteria, but these criteria may not all hold the same importance in your evaluation. To correct for this, simply assign weights to criteria to quantify their relative importance.

Introducing Regression Methods

Machine learning algorithms of the regression variety were adopted from the statistics field in order to provide data scientists with a set of methods for describing and quantifying the relationships between variables in a dataset. Use regression techniques if you want to determine the strength of correlation between variables in your data.

WARNING

As for using regression to predict future values from historical values, feel free to do it, but be careful: Regression methods assume a cause-and-effect relationship between variables, but present circumstances are always subject to flux. Predicting future values from historical ones will generate incorrect results when present circumstances change.

In this section, I tell you all about linear regression, logistic regression, and the ordinary least squares method.

Linear regression

Linear regression is a machine learning method you can use to describe and quantify the relationship between your target variable, y — the *predictant,* in statistics lingo — and the dataset features you've chosen to use as predictor variables (commonly designated as *dataset X* in machine learning). When you use just one variable as your predictor, linear regression is as simple as the middle school algebra formula $y = mx + b$. A classic example of linear regression is its usage in predicting home prices, as shown in Figure 4-6. You can also use linear regression to quantify correlations between several variables in a dataset — called *multiple linear regression*. Before getting too excited about using linear regression, though, make sure you've considered its limitations:

» Linear regression works with only numerical variables, not categorical ones.

» If your dataset has missing values, it will cause problems. Be sure to address your missing values before attempting to build a linear regression model.

» If your data has outliers present, your model will produce inaccurate results. Check for outliers before proceeding.

» The linear regression model assumes that a linear relationship exists between dataset features and the target variable.

» The linear regression model assumes that all features are independent of each other.

» Prediction errors, or *residuals,* should be normally distributed.

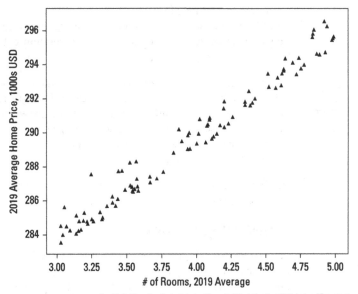

Credit: Python for Data Science Essential Training Part 2, LinkedIn.com

FIGURE 4-6: Linear regression used to predict home prices based on the number of rooms in a house.

Don't forget dataset size! A good rule of thumb is that you should have at least 20 observations per predictive feature if you expect to generate reliable results using linear regression.

Logistic regression

Logistic regression is a machine learning method you can use to estimate values for a categorical target variable based on your selected features. Your target variable should be numeric and should contain values that describe the target's class — or category. One cool aspect of logistic regression is that, in addition to predicting the class of observations in your target variable, it indicates the probability for each of its estimates. Though logistic regression is like linear regression, its requirements are simpler, in that:

>> There doesn't need to be a linear relationship between the features and target variable.

>> Residuals don't have to be normally distributed.

>> Predictive features aren't required to have a normal distribution.

When deciding whether logistic regression is a good choice for you, consider the following limitations:

>> Missing values should be treated or removed.

>> Your target variable must be binary or ordinal.

   Binary classification assigns a 1 for "yes" and a 0 for "no."

>> Predictive features should be independent of each other.

Logistic regression requires a greater number of observations than linear regression to produce a reliable result. The rule of thumb is that you should have at least 50 observations per predictive feature if you expect to generate reliable results.

Predicting survivors on the *Titanic* is the classic practice problem for newcomers to learn logistic regression. You can practice it and see lots of examples of this problem worked out over on Kaggle (www.kaggle.com/c/titanic).

Ordinary least squares regression methods

Ordinary least squares (OLS) is a statistical method that fits a linear regression line to a dataset. With OLS, you do this by squaring the vertical distance values that describe the distances between the data points and the best-fit line, adding up those squared distances, and then adjusting the placement of the best-fit line so that the summed squared distance value is minimized. Use OLS if you want to construct a function that's a close approximation to your data.

REMEMBER

As always, don't expect the actual value to be identical to the value predicted by the regression. Values predicted by the regression are simply estimates that are most similar to the actual values in the model.

OLS is particularly useful for fitting a regression line to models containing more than one independent variable. In this way, you can use OLS to estimate the target from dataset features.

WARNING

When using OLS regression methods to fit a regression line that has more than one independent variable, two or more of the variables may be interrelated. When two or more independent variables are strongly correlated with each other, this is called *multicollinearity*. Multicollinearity tends to adversely affect the reliability of the variables as predictors when they're examined apart from one another. Luckily, however, multicollinearity doesn't decrease the overall predictive reliability of the model when it's considered collectively.

Detecting Outliers

Many statistical and machine learning approaches assume that your data has no outliers. Outlier removal is an important part of preparing your data for analysis. In this section, you see a variety of methods you can use to discover outliers in your data.

Analyzing extreme values

Outliers are data points with values that are significantly different from the majority of data points comprising a variable. It's important to find and remove outliers because, left untreated, they skew variable distribution, make variance appear falsely high, and cause a misrepresentation of intervariable correlations.

You can use outlier detection to spot anomalies that represent fraud, equipment failure, or cybersecurity attacks. In other words, outlier detection is a data preparation method and an analytical method in its own right.

Outliers fall into the following three categories:

>> **Point:** Point outliers are data points with anomalous values compared to the normal range of values in a feature.

>> **Contextual:** Contextual outliers are data points that are anomalous only within a specific context. To illustrate, if you're inspecting weather station data from January in Orlando, Florida, and you see a temperature reading of 23°F, this would be quite anomalous because the average temperature there is 70°F in January. But consider if you were looking at data from January at a weather station in Anchorage, Alaska — a temperature reading of 23°F in this context isn't anomalous at all.

>> **Collective:** These outliers appear nearby one another, all having similar values that are anomalous to the majority of values in the feature.

You can detect outliers using either a univariate or a multivariate approach, as spelled out in the next two sections.

Detecting outliers with univariate analysis

Univariate outlier detection is where you look at features in your dataset and inspect them individually for anomalous values. You can choose from two simple methods for doing this:

>> Tukey outlier labeling

>> Tukey box plotting

Tukey box plotting is an exploratory data analysis technique that's useful for visualizing the distribution of data within a numeric variable by visualizing that distribution with quartiles. As you may guess, the Tukey box plot was named after its inventor, John Tukey, an American mathematician who did most of his work back in the 1960s and 1970s. Tukey outlier labeling refers to labeling data points (that lie beyond the minimum and maximum extremes of a box plot) as outliers.

Using the Tukey method to manually calculate, identify, and label outliers is cumbersome, but if you want to do it, the trick is to look at how far the minimum and maximum values are from the 25th and 75th percentiles. The distance between the first quartile (at 25 percent) and the third quartile (at 75 percent) is called the *inter-quartile range* (IQR), and it describes the data's spread. When you look at a variable, consider its spread, its Q1/Q3 values, and its minimum and maximum values to decide whether the variable is suspect for outliers.

TIP

Here's a good rule of thumb:

$$a = Q1 - 1.5 * IQR$$

and

$$b = Q3 + 1.5 * IQR$$

If your minimum value is less than a, or your maximum value is greater than b, the variable probably has outliers.

On the other hand, it's quite easy to generate a Tukey box plot and spot outliers using Python or R. Each box plot has whiskers that are set at 1.5 * IQR. Any values that lie beyond these whiskers are outliers. Figure 4-7 shows outliers as they appear within a Tukey box plot that was generated in Python.

Detecting outliers with multivariate analysis

Sometimes outliers show up only within combinations of data points from disparate variables. These outliers wreak havoc on machine learning algorithms, so it's important to detect and remove them. You can use multivariate analysis of outliers to do this. A multivariate approach to outlier detection involves considering two or more variables at a time and inspecting them together for outliers. You can use one of several methods:

» A scatter-plot matrix
» Box plotting

- » Density-based spatial clustering of applications with noise (DBScan), as discussed in Chapter 5
- » Principal component analysis (PCA), as shown in Figure 4-8

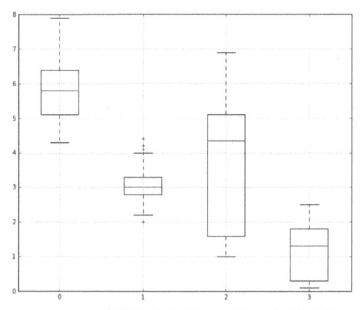

Credit: Python for Data Science Essential Training Part 1, LinkedIn.com

FIGURE 4-7: Spotting outliers with a Tukey box plot.

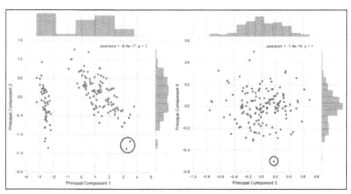

Credit: Python for Data Science Essential Training Part 2, LinkedIn.com

FIGURE 4-8: Using PCA to spot outliers.

Introducing Time Series Analysis

A *time series* is just a collection of data on attribute values over time. Time series analysis is performed to predict future instances of the measure based on the past observational data. To forecast or predict future values from data in your dataset, use time series techniques.

Identifying patterns in time series

Time series exhibit specific patterns. Take a look at Figure 4-9 to gain a better understanding of what these patterns are all about. *Constant* time series remain at roughly the same level over time but are subject to some random error. In contrast, *trended* series show a stable linear movement up or down. Whether constant or trended, time series may also sometimes exhibit *seasonality* — predictable, cyclical fluctuations that reoccur seasonally through-out a year. As an example of seasonal time series, consider how many businesses show increased sales during the holiday season.

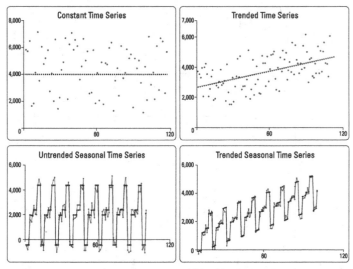

FIGURE 4-9: A comparison of patterns exhibited by time series.

If you're including seasonality in your model, incorporate it in the quarterly, monthly, or even biannual period — wherever it's appropriate. Time series may show *nonstationary processes* — unpredictable cyclical behavior that isn't related to seasonality and that results from economic or industry-wide conditions instead. Because they're not predictable, nonstationary processes can't be forecasted. You must transform nonstationary data to stationary data before moving forward with an evaluation.

Take a look at the solid lines shown earlier, in Figure 4-9. These represent the mathematical models used to forecast points in the time series. The mathematical models shown represent good, precise forecasts because they're a close fit to the actual data. The actual data contains some random error, making it impossible to forecast perfectly.

TIP

For help getting started with time series within the context of the R programming language, be sure to visit the companion website to this book (https://businessgrowth.ai), where you'll find a free training and coding demonstration of time series data visualization in R.

Modeling univariate time series data

Similar to how multivariate analysis is the analysis of relationships between multiple variables, *univariate analysis* is the quantitative analysis of only one variable at a time. When you model univariate time series, you're modeling time series changes that represent changes in a single variable over time.

Autoregressive moving average (ARMA) is a class of forecasting methods that you can use to predict future values from current and historical data. As its name implies, the family of ARMA models combines *autoregression techniques* (analyses that assume that previous observations are good predictors of future values and perform an autoregression analysis to forecast for those future values) and *moving average techniques* (models that measure the level of the constant time series and then update the forecast model if any changes are detected). If you're looking for a simple model or a model that will work for only a small dataset, the ARMA model isn't a good fit for your needs. An alternative in this case may be to just stick with simple linear regression. In Figure 4-10, you can see that the model forecast data and the actual data are a close fit.

REMEMBER

To use the ARMA model for reliable results, you need to have at least 50 observations.

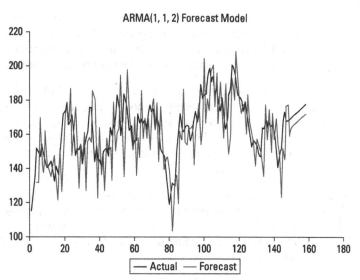

FIGURE 4-10: An example of an ARMA forecast model.

IN THIS CHAPTER

» Understanding the basics of clustering, classification, and other grouping algorithms

» Clustering your data with the *k*-means algorithm and kernel density estimation

» Choosing between decision trees and random forests

» Getting to know hierarchical and neighborhood clustering algorithms

» Working through nearest neighbor algorithms

Chapter **5**

Grouping Your Way into Accurate Predictions

When it comes to making predictions from data, grouping techniques can be a simple and powerful way to generate valuable insights quickly. Although grouping methods tend to be relatively simple, you can choose from quite a few approaches. In this chapter, I introduce you to classification, and clustering algorithms, as well as decision trees and random forests.

Data scientists use *clustering* to help them divide their unlabeled data into subsets. If they're starting with labeled data, they can use *classification methods* to build predictive models that they can then use to forecast the classification of future observations. Classification is a form of *supervised machine learning* — the classification algorithm essentially learns from your labeled data.

Though the basics behind clustering and classification seem relatively easy to understand at first, things get tricky fast when you get into using some of the more advanced algorithms.

In this chapter, I start you out with the simplest approach — clustering — and then lightly touch on decision trees and random forests before I help you, lastly, tackle instance-based learning classification algorithms.

Starting with Clustering Basics

To grasp advanced methods for use in clustering your data, first take a few moments to grasp the basics that underlie all forms of clustering. Clustering is a form of *machine learning* — the machine in this case is your computer, and *learning* refers to an algorithm that's repeated over and over until a certain set of predetermined conditions is met. Learning algorithms are generally run until the point that the final analysis results won't change, no matter how many additional times the algorithm is passed over the data.

Clustering is one of the two main types of machine learning: unsupervised machine learning. In *unsupervised machine learning,* the data in the dataset is unlabeled. Because the data is unlabeled, the algorithms must use inferential methods to discover patterns, relationships, and correlations within the raw dataset. To put clustering through its paces, I want to use a readily available sample dataset from the World Bank's open datasets on country income and education. This data shows the percentage of income earned by the bottom 10 percent of the population in each country and the percentage of children who complete primary school in each country.

WARNING

In datasets about the percentage of children who complete primary school, some are reported at more than 100 percent. That's because some countries count this statistic at different ages, but the data was *normalized* so that the percentage distribution is proportionally scaled across the range of countries represented in the dataset. In other words, although the total scale exceeds 100 percent, the values have been normalized so that they're proportional to one another and you're getting an apples-to-apples comparison. Thus, the fact that some countries report completion rates greater than 100 percent has no adverse effect on the analysis you make in this chapter.

Getting to know clustering algorithms

You use clustering algorithms to subdivide unlabeled datasets into clusters of observations that are most similar for a pre-defined feature. If you have a dataset that describes multiple features about a set of observations and you want to group your observations by their feature similarities, use clustering algorithms.

Over on the companion website to this book (https://business growth.ai), you'll find a free training-and-coding demonstration of how to use clustering in Python for a popular use case — customer profiling and segmentation.

You can choose from various clustering methods, depending on how you want your dataset to be divided. The two main types of clustering algorithms are

>> **Partitional:** Algorithms that create only a single set of clusters

>> **Hierarchical:** Algorithms that create separate sets of nested clusters, each in its own hierarchical level

You can read about both approaches later in this chapter, but for now, start by looking at Figure 5-1, a simple scatterplot of the Country Income and Education datasets.

In unsupervised clustering, you start with this data and then proceed to divide it into subsets. These subsets, called *clusters*, are composed of observations that are most similar to one another. In Figure 5-1, it appears that the scatterplot has at least two clusters, and probably three — one at the bottom with low income and education, and then the high-education countries look like they may be split between low and high incomes.

Figure 5-2 shows the result of *eyeballing* (making a visual estimate of) clusters in this dataset.

Although you can generate visual estimates of clusters, you can achieve much more accurate results when dealing with much larger datasets by using algorithms to generate clusters for you. Visual estimation is a rough method that's useful only on smaller datasets of minimal complexity. Algorithms produce exact, repeatable results, and you can use algorithms to generate clusters from multiple dimensions of data within your dataset.

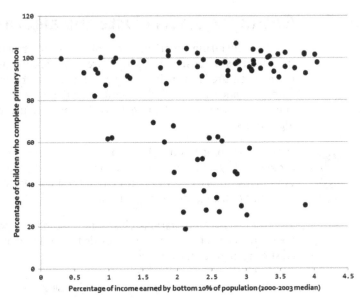

FIGURE 5-1: A simple scatterplot.

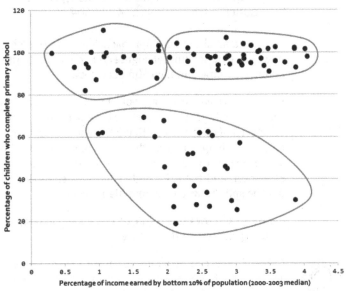

FIGURE 5-2: A simple scatterplot, showing eyeballed estimations of clustering.

Clustering algorithms are appropriate in situations where the following characteristics are true:

- ≫ You know and understand the dataset you're analyzing.

- ≫ Before running the clustering algorithm, you don't have an exact idea of the nature of the subsets (clusters). Often, you don't even know how many subsets are in the dataset before you run the algorithm.

- ≫ The subsets (clusters) are determined by only the single dataset you're analyzing.

- ≫ Your goal is to determine a model that describes the subsets in a single dataset and only this dataset.

TIP

If you add more data to your dataset after you've already built the model, be sure to rebuild the model from scratch to produce more complete and accurate model results.

Examining clustering similarity metrics

Clustering is based on calculating the similarity or difference between two observations. If your dataset is *numeric* (composed of only numerical features) and can be portrayed on an *n*-dimensional plot, you can use various geometric metrics to scale your multidimensional data.

REMEMBER

An n-*dimensional plot* is a multidimensional scatterplot that you can use to plot *n* number of dimensions of data.

Here are some popular geometric metrics, used for calculating distances between observations:

- ≫ **Euclidean:** A measure of the distance between points plotted on a Euclidean plane.

- ≫ **Manhattan:** A measure of the distance between points where distance is calculated as the sum of the absolute value of the differences between two points' Cartesian coordinates.

- ≫ **Minkowski distance:** A generalization of the Euclidean and Manhattan distance metrics. Quite often, these metrics can be used interchangeably.

- ≫ **Cosine similarity:** The cosine metric measures the similarity of two data points based on their orientation, as determined by calculating the cosine of the angle between them.

Lastly, for nonnumeric data, you can use metrics like the *Jaccard distance metric,* an index that compares the number of features that two observations have in common. For example, to illustrate a Jaccard distance, look at these two text strings:

```
Saint Louis de Ha-ha, Quebec
St-Louis de Ha!Ha!, QC
```

What features do these text strings have in common? And what features are different between them? The Jaccard metric generates a numerical index value that quantifies the similarity between text strings.

Identifying Clusters in Your Data

You can use many different algorithms for clustering, but the speed and robustness of the *k*-means algorithm make it a popular choice among experienced data scientists. As alternatives, kernel density estimation methods, hierarchical algorithms, and neighborhood algorithms are also available to help you identify clusters in your dataset.

Clustering with the k-means algorithm

The k-*means* clustering algorithm is a simple, fast, unsupervised learning algorithm that you can use to predict groupings within a dataset. For getting started with *k*-means clustering, you first need to be familiar with the concept of centroid. A *centroid* is the most representative point within any given cluster group. With *k*-means, you define the number of centroids the model should find as it generates its prediction. The *number of centroids* is represented by *k*, and the clusters are formed by calculating the nearest mean values to those centroids, measured by the Euclidean distance between observations.

WARNING

Because the features of a dataset are usually on different scales, the difference of scales can distort the results of this distance calculation. To avoid this problem, scale your variables before using *k*-means to predict data groupings.

The quality of the clusters is heavily dependent on the correctness of the *k* value you specify. If your data is two- or three-dimensional, a plausible range of *k* values may be visually determinable. In the eyeballed approximation of clustering from the World Bank Income and Education data scatterplot (refer to Figure 5-2), a visual estimation of the k value would equate to three clusters, or $k = 3$.

When defining the k value, it may be possible to choose the number of centroids by looking at a scatterplot (if your dataset is two- or three-dimensional) or by looking for obvious, significant groupings within your dataset's variables. You can pick the number of centroids based on the number of groupings that you know exist in the dataset or by the number of groupings that you want to exist in the dataset. Whatever the case, use your subjective knowledge about the dataset when choosing the number of clusters to be modeled.

If your dataset has more than three dimensions, however, you can use computational methods to generate a good value for k. One such method is the *silhouette coefficient* (a method that calculates the average distance of each point from all other points in a cluster and then compares that value with the average distance to every point in every other cluster). Luckily, because the k-means algorithm is efficient, it doesn't require much computer processing power and you can easily calculate this coefficient for a wide range of k values.

The k-means algorithm works by placing sample cluster centers on an n-dimensional plot and then evaluating whether moving them in any single direction would result in a new center with higher *density* — with more observations closer to it, in other words. The centers are moved from regions of lower density to regions of higher density until all centers are within a region of *local maximum density* (a true center of the cluster, where each cluster has a maximum number of data points closest to its cluster center). Whenever possible, try to place the centers yourself, manually. If that's impossible, simply place the centers randomly and run the algorithm several times to see how often you end up with the same clusters.

One weakness of the k-means algorithm is that it may produce incorrect results by placing cluster centers in areas of *local minimum density*. This happens when centers get lost in *low-density regions* (in other words, regions of the plot that have relatively few points plotted in them) and the algorithm-driven *directional movement* (the movement that's meant to increase point density) starts to bounce and oscillate between faraway clusters. In these cases, the center gets caught in a low-density space that's located between two high-point density zones. This results in erroneous clusters based around centers that converge in areas of low, local minimum density. Ironically, this happens most often when the underlying data is very well clustered, with tight, dense regions that are separated by wide, sparse areas.

TIP

Get hands-on experience with the free k-means clustering coding demo that's hosted on the companion website for this book: https://businessgrowth.ai.

TIP

To try things out for yourself, start clustering your data with the k-means methods by using either R's cluster package or Python's scikit-learn library. For more on R's cluster package, check out https://cran.r-project.org/web/packages/cluster/cluster.pdf; for more on scikit-learn, check out https://scikit-learn.org.

Estimating clusters with kernel density estimation

If the k-means algorithm doesn't appeal to you, one alternative way to identify clusters in your data is to use a density smoothing function instead. *Kernel density estimation* (KDE) is that smoothing method; it works by placing a *kernel* (a weighting function that's useful for quantifying density) on each data point in the dataset and then summing the kernels to generate a kernel density estimate for the overall region. Areas of greater point density will sum out with greater kernel density, and areas of lower point density will sum out with less kernel density.

Because kernel smoothing methods don't rely on cluster center placement and clustering techniques to estimate clusters, they don't exhibit a risk of generating erroneous clusters by placing centers in areas of local minimum density. Where k-means algorithms generate hard-lined definitions between points in different clusters, KDE generates a plot of gradual density change between observations. For this reason, it's a helpful aid when eyeballing clusters. Figure 5-3 shows what the World Bank Income and Education scatterplot looks like after KDE has been applied.

In Figure 5-3, you can see that the white spaces between clusters have been reduced. When you look at the figure, it's fairly obvious that you can see at least three clusters, and possibly more, if you want to allow for small clusters.

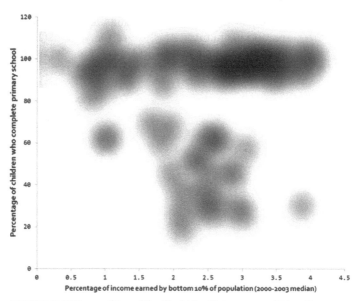

FIGURE 5-3: KDE smoothing of the World Bank's Income and Education data scatterplot.

Clustering with hierarchical algorithms

A hierarchical clustering algorithm is yet another alternative to k-means clustering. In comparison to k-means clustering, the hierarchical clustering algorithm is a slower, clunkier unsupervised clustering algorithm. It predicts groupings within a dataset by calculating the distance and generating a link between each singular observation and its nearest neighbor. It then uses those distances to predict subgroups within a dataset. If you're carrying out a statistical study or analyzing biological or environmental data, hierarchical clustering may be your ideal machine learning solution.

To visually inspect the results of your hierarchical clustering, generate a *dendrogram* (a visualization tool that depicts the similarities and branching between groups in a data cluster). You can use several different algorithms to build a dendrogram, and the algorithm you choose dictates where and how branching occurs within the clusters. Additionally, dendrograms can be built either *bottom-up* (by assembling pairs of points and then aggregating them into larger and larger groups) or *top-down* (by starting with the full dataset and splitting it into smaller and smaller groups).

Looking at the dendrogram results makes it easier to decide the appropriate number of clusters for your dataset. In the dendrogram example shown in Figure 5-4, the underlying dataset appears to have either three or four clusters.

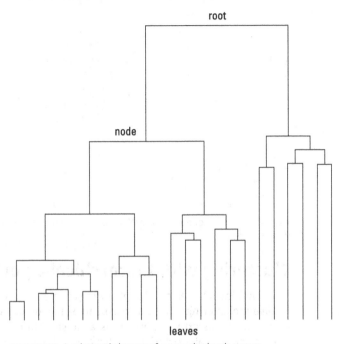

FIGURE 5-4: A schematic layout of a sample dendrogram.

In hierarchical clustering, the distance between observations is measured in three different ways: Euclidean, Manhattan, or Cosine. Additionally, linkage is formed by three different methods: Ward, Complete, and Average. When deciding what distance and linkage parameters to use, trial-and-error is an easy approach. Just try each combination and then compare all your model results. Go with the model that produces the most accurate prediction.

Hierarchical clustering algorithms require more computing resources than k-means algorithms because, with each iteration of hierarchical clustering, many observations must be compared to many other observations. The benefit, however, is that hierarchical clustering algorithms are not subject to errors caused by center convergence at areas of local minimum density (as exhibited with the k-means clustering algorithms).

If you're working with a large dataset, watch out! Hierarchical clustering will probably be *way* too slow.

If you want to get started working with hierarchical clustering algorithms, check out R's hclust package or (again) Python's scikit-learn library. (If you're curious about hclust, check out this page: https://stat.ethz.ch/R-manual/R-patched/library/stats/html/hclust.html.)

Neither k-means nor hierarchical clustering algorithms perform well when clusters are *nonglobular* (a configuration where some points in a cluster are closer to points in a different cluster than they are to points in the center of their own cluster). If your dataset shows nonglobular clustering, you can use neighborhood clustering algorithms, like DBScan, to determine whether each point is closer to its neighbors in the same cluster or closer to its neighboring observations in other clusters. Figure 5-5 shows an example of using the DBScan neighborhood clustering algorithm to detect outliers in the classical practice dataset called "Iris," and the next section covers neighborhood clustering in greater detail.

Dabbling in the DBScan neighborhood

Density-based spatial clustering of applications with noise (DBScan) is an unsupervised learning method that works by clustering *core samples* (dense areas of a dataset) while simultaneously demarking *noncore samples* (portions of the dataset that are comparatively sparse). It's a neighborhood clustering algorithm that's ideal for examining two or more variables together to identify outliers. It's particularly useful for identifying *collective outliers* (outliers that appear nearby to one another, all having similar values that are anomalous to most values in the variable). Figure 5-5 shows DBScan at work.

With DBScan, you take an iterative, trial-and-error approach to find the ideal number of outliers for inspection. When experimenting with the DBScan model, outliers should comprise 5 percent or less of the dataset's observations. You must adjust the model parameters until you've isolated this small select group of observations.

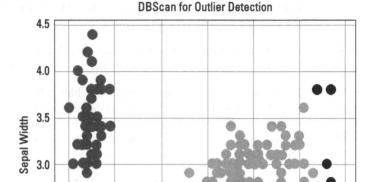

Credit: Python for Data Science Essential Training Part 2, LinkedIn.com

FIGURE 5-5: Using DBScan to detect outliers (in black) within the Iris dataset.

Neighborhood clustering algorithms are generally effective, but they're subject to the following two weaknesses:

>> **Neighborhood clustering can be computationally expensive.** With every iteration of this method, every data point may have to be compared to every other data point in the dataset.

>> **With neighborhood clustering, you may have to provide the model with empirical parameter values for expected cluster size and cluster density.** If you guess either of these parameters incorrectly, the algorithm misidentifies clusters, and you must start the whole long process over again to fix the problem. If you choose to use the DBScan method, you're required to specify these parameters. (As an alternative, you could try the average nearest neighbor and *k*-nearest neighbor algorithms, discussed later in this chapter.)

To avoid making poor guesses for the cluster size and cluster density parameters, you can first use a quick k-means algorithm to determine plausible values.

Categorizing Data with Decision Tree and Random Forest Algorithms

In cases where clustering algorithms fail, decision tree and random forest algorithms may just offer you a perfect alternative machine learning solution. At certain times, you can get stuck trying to cluster and classify data from a non-numerical dataset. It's times like these that you can use a decision tree model to help cluster and classify your data correctly.

A *decision tree* algorithm works by developing a set of yes-or-no rules that you can follow for new data to see exactly how it will be characterized by the model. But you must be careful when using decision tree models, because they run the high risk of *error propagation*, which occurs whenever one of the model rules is incorrect. Errors are generated in the results of decisions that are made based on that incorrect rule, and then propagated through every other subsequent decision made along that branch of the tree.

To illustrate this type of algorithm, consider a dataset that's often used in machine learning demonstrations — the list of passenger names from the *Titanic.* Using a simple decision tree model, you can predict that if a passenger were female or were a male child with a large family, that person probably survived the catastrophe. Figure 5-6 illustrates this determination.

Lastly, random forest algorithms are a slower but more powerful alternative. Instead of building a tree from the data, the algorithm creates random trees and then determines which one best classifies the testing data. This method eliminates the risk of error propagation that is inherent in decision tree models.

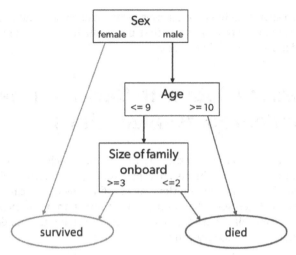

FIGURE 5-6: A decision tree model predicts survival rates from the *Titanic* catastrophe.

Drawing a Line between Clustering and Classification

The purpose of both clustering and classification algorithms is to make sense of, and extract value from, large sets of structured and unstructured data. If you're working with huge volumes of unstructured data, it only makes sense to try to partition the data into some sort of logical groupings before trying to analyze it. Both clustering and classification methods allow you to take a sweeping glance of your data all at once and then form some logical structures based on what you find there, before digging deeper into the nuts-and-bolts analysis.

Although a plain-vanilla clustering algorithm — like the k-means method discussed earlier in this chapter — can help you predict subgroups from within *unlabeled* datasets, there's way more to life than plain vanilla. I think it's about time to take things one step further, by exploring how we can make predictions by grouping *labeled* data instead. Enter instance-based learning classifiers!

Introducing instance-based learning classifiers

Instance-based learning classifiers are supervised, lazy learners — they have no training phase, and they simply memorize training data to predict classifications for new data points. This type of classifier looks at *instances* (observations within a dataset) and, for each new observation, the classifier searches the training data for observations that are most similar and then classifies the new observation based on its similarity to instances in the training set. Instance-based classifiers include

>> *k*-nearest neighbor (*k*-NN)

>> Self-organizing maps

>> Locally weighted learning

If you're unsure about your dataset's distribution, instance-based classifiers may be a good option, but first make sure that you know their limitations. These classifiers aren't well-suited for

>> *Noisy data* (data with unexplainable random variation)

>> Datasets with unimportant or irrelevant features

>> Datasets with missing values

To simplify this introduction as much as possible, I stick to explaining the *k*-NN classification algorithm. The concepts involved in *k*-NN are a bit tricky, though, so first I introduce you to the simpler average nearest neighbor methods before going into the *k*-NN approach.

Getting to know classification algorithms

You may have heard of classification and thought that it's the same concept as clustering. Many people do, but this isn't the case. In *classification*, your data is *labeled*, so before you analyze it, you already know the number of classes into which it should be grouped. You also already know which class you want assigned to each data point. In contrast, with *clustering* methods, your data is *unlabeled*, so you have no predefined concept of how many clusters are appropriate. You must rely on the clustering algorithms to sort and cluster the data in the most appropriate way.

With classification algorithms, you use what you know about an existing labeled dataset to generate a predictive model for classifying future observations. If your goal is to use your dataset and its known subsets to build a model for predicting the categorization of future observations, you'll want to use classification algorithms. When implementing supervised classification, you already know your dataset's *labels* — the criteria you use to subset observations into classes. Classification helps you see how well your data fits into the dataset's predefined classes so that you can then build a predictive model for classifying future observations.

Figure 5-7 illustrates how it looks to classify the World Bank's Income and Education datasets geographically according to continent.

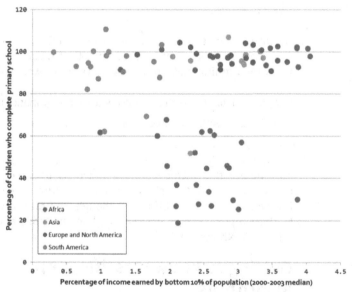

FIGURE 5-7: Using the Continent feature to classify World Bank data.

In Figure 5-7, you can see that, in some cases, the subsets you may identify with a clustering technique do correspond to the Continent category, but in other cases, they don't. For example, look at the lone Asian country in the middle of the African observations. That's Bhutan. You could use the data in this dataset to build a model that would predict a Continent class for incoming observations, but if you introduced a data point for a new country that showed statistics similar to those of Bhutan, the new country could be categorized as being part of either the Asian continent or the African continent, depending on how you define your model.

Now imagine a situation in which the original data doesn't include Bhutan and you use the model to predict Bhutan's continent as a new data point. In this scenario, the model would incorrectly predict that Bhutan is part of the African continent. This is an example of *model overfitting* — a situation in which a model is so tightly fit to its underlying dataset, as well as its noise or random error, that the model performs poorly as a predictor for new observations.

To avoid overfitting your models, divide the data into a training set and a test set. A typical ratio is to assign 70 percent (or more) of the data to the training set and the remaining 30 percent to the test set. Build your model with the training set, and then use the test set to evaluate the model by pretending that the test set observations are unknown. You can evaluate the accuracy of your model by comparing the classes assigned to the test set observations to the true classes of these observations.

Model overgeneralization can also be a problem. *Overgeneralization* is the opposite of overfitting: If you don't train a machine learning model enough, it will be underfit. As a result, it will make inaccurate, overly general predictions. Naturally, it follows that overly general models end up assigning every class a low degree of confidence. To illustrate model overgeneralization, consider again the World Bank Income and Education datasets. If the model used the presence of Bhutan to cast doubt on every new data point in its nearby vicinity, you'd end up with a wishy-washy model that treats all nearby points as African, but with a low probability. This model would be a poor predictive performer.

I can illustrate a good metaphor for overfitting and overgeneralization by using this well-known maxim:

> If it walks like a duck and talks like a duck, then it's a duck.

Overfitting would turn the maxim into this statement:

> It's a duck if, and only if, it walks and quacks exactly in the ways that I have personally observed a duck to walk and quack. Because I've never observed the way an Australian

spotted duck walks and quacks, an Australian spotted duck must not really be a duck at all.

In contrast, overgeneralization would say:

If it moves around on two legs and emits any high-pitched, nasal sound, it's a duck. Therefore, Fran Fine, who was Fran Drescher's character in the 1990s American sitcom *The Nanny*, must be a duck.

Be aware of the constant danger of overfitting and overgeneralization. Find a happy medium between the two.

REMEMBER

When classifying data, keep these two points in mind:

>> **Model predictions are only as good as the model's underlying data.** In the World Bank data example, it could be the case that, if other factors such as life expectancy or energy use per capita were added to the model, its predictive strength would increase.

>> **Model predictions are only as good as the categorization of the underlying dataset.** For example, what do you do with countries, like Russia, that span two continents? Do you distinguish North Africa from sub-Saharan Africa? Do you lump North America in with Europe because they tend to share similar features? Do you consider Central America to be part of North America or South America?

Making Sense of Data with Nearest Neighbor Analysis

At their core, nearest neighbor methods work by taking the value of an observation's attribute (or feature) — also called an *attribute value* — and then locating another observation whose attribute value is numerically nearest to it. Because the nearest neighbor technique is a classification method, you can use it to perform tasks as scientifically oriented as deducing the molecular structure of a vital human protein or uncovering key biological evolutionary relationships or as business-driven as designing recommendation engines for e-commerce sites or building predictive models for consumer transactions. The applications are limitless.

A good analogy for the nearest neighbor concept is illustrated in GPS technology. Imagine that you're in desperate need of a Starbucks iced latte but you have no idea where the nearest store is located. What to do? One easy solution is simply to ask your smartphone where the nearest Starbucks is located.

When you do that, the system looks for businesses named Starbucks within a reasonable proximity of your current location. After generating a results listing, the system reports back to you with the address of the Starbucks coffeehouse closest to your current location — the one that is your nearest neighbor, in other words.

As the term *nearest neighbor* implies, the primary purpose of a nearest neighbor analysis is to examine your dataset and find the observation that's quantitatively most similar to your observation. Note that similarity comparisons can be based on any quantitative attribute, whether that is distance, age, income, weight, or any other factor that can describe the observation you're investigating. The simplest comparative attribute is distance.

In my Starbucks analogy, the x, y, z coordinates of the store reported to you by your smartphone are the most similar to the x, y, z coordinates of your current location. In other words, its location is closest in actual physical distance. The quantitative *attribute* being compared is distance, your current location is the *observation,* and the reported Starbucks coffeehouse is the *most similar observation.*

REMEMBER

Modern nearest neighbor analyses are almost always performed using computational algorithms. The nearest neighbor algorithm is known as a *single-link algorithm* — an algorithm that merges clusters if the clusters share between them at least one *connective edge* (a shared boundary line, in other words). In the following sections, you can learn the basics of the average nearest neighbor algorithm and the k-nearest neighbor algorithm.

Classifying Data with Average Nearest Neighbor Algorithms

Average nearest neighbor algorithms are basic yet powerful classification algorithms. They're useful for finding and classifying observations that are most similar on average. Average nearest neighbor algorithms are used in pattern recognition, in chemical and biological structural analysis, and in spatial data modeling. They're most often used in biology, chemistry, engineering, and geosciences.

In this section, you can find out how to use average nearest neighbor algorithms to compare multiple attributes between observations and, subsequently, identify which of your observations are most similar. You can also find out how to use average nearest neighbor algorithms to identify significant patterns in the dataset.

The purpose of using an average nearest neighbor algorithm is to classify observations based on the average of the arithmetic distances between them. If your goal is to identify and group observations by average similarity, the average nearest neighbor algorithm is a useful way to do that.

With respect to nearest neighbor classifiers, a dataset is composed of observations, each of which has an x- and y-variable. An x-variable represents the input value, or *feature*, and the y-variable represents the data label, or target variable. To keep all these terms straight, consider the following example.

Suppose your friendly neighborhood business analyst, Business Analyst Stu, is using average nearest neighbor algorithms to perform a classification analysis of datasets in his organization's database. Stu is comparing employees based on the following five features:

>> Age
>> Number of children
>> Annual income
>> Seniority
>> Eligibility to retire

Here you can see that each employee in Stu's organization is represented by a five-dimensional *tuple* — a finite ordered list (or *sequence*):

» **Employee Mike:** (34, 1, 120000, 9, 0)

» **Employee Liz:** (42, 0, 90000, 5, 0)

» **Employee Jin:** (22, 0, 60000, 2, 0)

» **Employee Mary:** (53, 3, 180000, 30, 1)

These tuples were created from the data in the dataset shown in Table 5-1. Each tuple consists of data on the following five features: Age, Number of Children, Annual Income, Seniority, and Eligibility to Retire as predictive features. Business Analyst Stu calculates the average arithmetic differences between each of the employees. Figure 5-8 shows the calculated distances between each of the employees.

TABLE 5-1 **Business Analyst Stu's Employee Data**

Employee Name	Age	Number of Children	Annual Income	Seniority	Eligibility to Retire
Mike	34	1	$120,000	9	0
Liz	42	0	$90,000	5	0
Jin	22	0	$60,000	2	0
Mary	53	3	$180,000	30	1

After Business Analyst Stu has this arithmetic measure of distance between the employees, he finds the *average nearest neighbor* by taking an average of these separation distances. Figure 5-9 shows that average similarity.

Stu then groups the employees by the average separation distance between them. Because the average separation distance values between Mike, Liz, and Jin are the smallest, they're grouped into class 0. Mary's average separation distances are quite unlike the others, so she's put into her own class — Class 1.

Mike	34	1	120000	9
Liz	42	0	90000	5
Distance between employees	**8**	**1**	**30000**	**4**
Mike	34	1	120000	9
Jin	22	0	60000	2
Distance between employees	**12**	**1**	**60000**	**7**
Mike	34	1	120000	9
Mary	53	3	180000	30
Distance between employees	**19**	**2**	**60000**	**21**
Liz	42	0	90000	5
Jin	22	0	60000	2
Distance between employees	**20**	**0**	**30000**	**3**
Liz	42	0	90000	5
Mary	53	3	180000	30
Distance between employees	**11**	**3**	**90000**	**25**
Jin	22	0	60000	2
Mary	53	3	180000	30
Distance between employees	**31**	**3**	**120000**	**28**

FIGURE 5-8: The distances between the employees' tuples.

Finding Average Similarities	
Average Distance (Mike - Liz)	
Average Distance Value - (Average of 8, 1, 30000, 4)	7503.25
Average Distance (Mike - Jin)	
Average Distance Value - (Average of 12, 1, 60000, 7)	15005
Average Distance (Mike - Mary)	
Average Distance Value - (Average of 19, 2, 60000, 21)	15010.5
Average Distance (Liz - Jin)	
Average Distance Value - (Average of 20, 0, 30000, 3)	7505.75
Average Distance (Liz - Mary)	
Average Distance Value - (Average of 11, 3, 90000, 25)	22509.75
Average Distance (Jin - Mary)	
Average Distance Value - (Average of)	30015.5

FIGURE 5-9: Finding the average similarity between employees.

Does this make sense? Well, you're working with a labeled dataset and you can see that the attribute Eligibility to Retire assumes only one of two possible values. So, yes. If the algorithm predicts two classifications within the data, that's a reasonable prediction. Plus, if Stu gets new incoming data points that are unlabeled with respect to a person's eligibility to retire, he could probably use this algorithm to predict for that eligibility, based on the other four features.

Classifying with K-Nearest Neighbor Algorithms

The best way to define a k-nearest neighbor is to call it a supervised machine learning classifier that uses the observations it memorizes from within a test dataset to predict classifications for new, unlabeled observations. k-NN makes its predictions based on *similarity* — the more similar the training observations are to the new, incoming observations, the more likely it is that the classifier will assign them both the same class. k-NN works best if the dataset is

>> Low on noise

>> Free of outliers

>> Labeled

>> Composed only of relevant selected features

>> Composed of distinguishable groups

WARNING

If you're working with a large dataset, you may want to avoid using k-NN, because it will probably take way too long to make predictions from larger datasets.

TIP

Over on the companion website to this book (https://business growth.ai), you'll find a free training-and-coding demonstration of how to build a quick-and-easy k-nearest neighbor classifier in Python.

In the larger context of machine learning, k-NN (like all instance-based learning classifiers) is known as a *lazy* machine learning algorithm — in other words, it has little to no training phase. It simply memorizes training data and then uses that information as the basis on which to classify new observations. The goal of the k-NN is to estimate the class of the query point P based on the classes of its k-nearest neighbors.

The k-NN algorithm is a generalization of the nearest neighbor algorithm. Instead of considering the nearest neighbor, you consider k numbers of nearest neighbors from within a dataset that contains n number of data points — k defines how many nearest neighbors will have an influence on the classification process. In k-NN, the classifier classifies the query point P per the classification labels found in a majority of k-nearest points surrounding the query point.

If you know little about the distribution of your dataset, k-NN is definitely a good classification method for you to use. What's more, if you do have a solid idea about your dataset's distribution and *feature selection criteria* (the criteria you're using to identify and remove noise in the dataset), you can leverage this information to create significant enhancements in the algorithm's performance.

REMEMBER

Even though k-NN is among the simplest and most easy-to-implement classification methods, it nevertheless yields competitive results when compared to some of the more sophisticated machine learning methods. Probably because of its simplicity and the competitive results it provides, the k-NN algorithm has been ranked among the top ten most influential data mining algorithms by the academic research community.

Understanding how the k-nearest neighbor algorithm works

To use k-NN, you simply need to pick a query point — usually called P — in the sample dataset and then compute the k-nearest neighbors to this point. The query point P is classified with a label that's the same as the label of most k-nearest points that surround it. (Figure 5-10 gives a bird's-eye view of the process.)

REMEMBER

k-nearest neighbors are quantified by either distance or similarity based on another quantitative attribute.

Consider the following example: A dataset is given by [1, 1, 4, 3, 5, 2, 6, 2, 4], and point P is equal to 5. Figure 5-10 shows how k-NN would be applied to this dataset. By specifying that k is equal to 3, the figure shows that, based on distance, there are three nearest neighbors to the point 5. Those neighbors are 4, 4, and 6. So, based on the k-NN algorithm, query point P will be classified as 4 because 4 is the majority number in the k number of points nearest to it. Similarly, k-NN continues defining other query points using the same majority principle.

REMEMBER

When using k-NN, it's crucial to choose a k value that minimizes *noise* (unexplainable random variation). At the same time, you must choose a k value that includes sufficient data points in the selection process. If the data points aren't uniformly distributed, it's generally harder to predetermine a good *k* value. Be careful to select an optimum *k* value for each dataset you're analyzing.

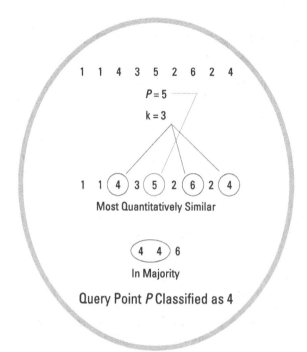

TIP

Large *k* values tend to produce less noise and more *boundary smoothing* (clearer definition and less overlap) between classes than small *k* values do.

Knowing when to use the k-nearest neighbor algorithm

k-NN is particularly useful for *multi-label learning* — supervised learning where the algorithm is applied so that it automatically *learns from* (detects patterns in) multiple sets of instances. Each of these sets could potentially have several classes of its own. With multi-label learning, the algorithm learns to predict multiple class labels for each new instance it encounters.

The problem with *k*-NN is that it takes a lot longer than other classification methods to classify a sample. Nearest neighbor classifier performance depends on calculating the distance function, as well as on the value of the neighborhood parameter k. You can try to speed things up by specifying optimal values for k and n.

Exploring common applications of k-nearest neighbor algorithms

k-NN is often used for internet database management purposes. In this capacity, k-NN is useful for website categorization, web page ranking, and other user dynamics across the web.

k-NN classification techniques are also quite beneficial in *customer relationship management* (CRM), a set of processes that ensure a business sustains improved relationships with its clients while simultaneously experiencing increased business revenues. Most CRM systems gain tremendous benefit from using k-NN to data-mine customer information to find patterns that are useful in boosting customer retention.

The method is so versatile that even if you're a small-business owner or a marketing department manager, you can easily use k-NN to boost your own marketing return on investment. Simply use k-NN to analyze your customer data for purchasing patterns, and then use those findings to customize marketing initiatives so that they're more exactly targeted for your customer base.

Solving Real-World Problems with Nearest Neighbor Algorithms

Nearest neighbor methods are used extensively to understand and create value from patterns in retail business data. In the following sections, I present two powerful cases where k-NN and average-NN algorithms are being used to simplify management and security in daily retail operations.

Seeing k-nearest neighbor algorithms in action

Techniques associated with k-nearest neighbor algorithms are often used for theft prevention in the modern retail business. Of course, you're accustomed to seeing closed-circuit television

(CCTV) cameras around almost every store you visit, but most people have no idea how the data gathered from these devices is being used.

Maybe you imagine someone in the back room resolutely monitoring these cameras for suspicious activity for hours at a time — and maybe that *is* how things were done in the past. But today a modern surveillance system is intelligent enough to analyze and interpret video data on its own, without the need for human assistance. The modern systems can now use k-nearest neighbor for visual pattern recognition to scan and detect hidden packages in the bottom bin of a shopping cart at checkout. If an object is detected that is an exact match with an object listed in the database, the price of the spotted product can even automatically be added to the customer's bill. Though this automated billing practice isn't used extensively now, the technology has been developed and is available for use.

Retail stores also use k-nearest neighbor to detect patterns in credit card use. Many new transaction-scrutinizing software applications use k-NN algorithms to analyze register data and spot unusual patterns that indicate suspicious activity. For example, if register data indicates that a lot of customer information is being entered manually rather than by automated scanning and swiping, it can indicate that the employee who's using that register is stealing a customer's personal information. Or, if register data indicates that a particular good is being returned or exchanged multiple times, it can indicate that employees are misusing the return policy or trying to make money from making fake returns.

Seeing average nearest neighbor algorithms in action

Average nearest neighbor algorithm classification and point pattern detection can be used in grocery retail to identify key patterns in customer purchasing behavior, and subsequently increase sales and customer satisfaction by anticipating customer behavior. Consider the following story.

As with other grocery stores, buyer behavior at (the fictional) Waldorf Food Co-op tends to follow fixed patterns. Managers have even commented on the odd fact that members of a particular age group tend to visit the store during the same particular time window, and they even tend to buy the same types of products.

One day, Manager Mike became extremely proactive and decided to hire a data scientist to analyze customer data and provide exact details about some recent trends that were noticeably odd. Data Scientist Danielle got in there and quickly uncovered a pattern among employed middle-aged male adults: They tended to visit the grocery store only during the weekends or at the end of the day on weekdays, and if they entered the store on a Thursday, they almost always bought beer.

Armed with these facts, Manager Mike quickly used this information to maximize beer sales on Thursday evenings by offering discounts, bundles, and specials. Not only was the store owner happy with the increased revenues, but Waldorf Food Co-op's male customers were also happy because they got more of what they wanted, when they wanted it.

Chapter **6**

Coding Up Data Insights and Decision Engines

ata science involves the skillful application of math, coding, and subject matter expertise in ways that allow data scientists to generate reliable and accurate predictions from data. In this chapter, I introduce you to the fundamental concepts of programming with Python (such as data types, functions, and classes). The machine learning models you build with this language can serve as the *decision engines* within artificial intelligence (AI) software as a service (SaaS) products you build for your company. I also introduce some of the best Python libraries for manipulating data, performing statistical computations, creating data visualizations, and completing other data science tasks.

Seeing Where Python Fits into Your Data Science Strategy

Would you be surprised to hear that not all data projects that are out there trying to turn a profit necessarily require data science? It may seem odd, but it's true! Think about LinkedIn for a second: Imagine how much less useful that platform would be if it didn't allow direct messaging between users. That feature directly improves the user experience, keeping users returning more often and keeping them more active on the platform for longer periods, thus increasing the overall profitability of the LinkedIn platform.

The longer users stay active on the platform and the more often they return, the more likely they are to generate revenues for the platform — either by subscribing to LinkedIn Learning or by using Open to Work, a LinkedIn designation that encourages recruiters to contact them. (With Open to Work, the contacting of users is paid for by the recruiter as a form of indirect monetization of users on the platform.) The popular LinkedIn Premium feature allows users to message others directly on the platform, regardless of whether they know them. All these monetization features rely directly on LinkedIn's direct messaging product. And do you know what it's built on? It's the data engineering technology called Apache Kafka. Not advanced machine learning models, not deep learning — just traditional, tried-and-tested data engineering (see Chapter 2).

But for those for-profit data projects that involve data science, you'll want to make sure you have a well-formed and effective data science strategy in place, governing project implementation. A *data science strategy* is a technical plan that maps out each and every element required to lead data science projects in ways that increase the profitability of a business. Because Python is the lifeblood by which data science produces predictive insights designed to increase profits, you'd be hard-pressed to find a place where they don't fit within an effective data science strategy.

Using Python for Data Science

Although popular programming languages like Java and C++ are good for developing stand-alone desktop applications, Python's versatility makes it an ideal programming language for processing, analyzing, and visualizing data. For this reason, Python has earned a reputation of excellence in the data science field, where it has been widely adopted over the past decade. Python's status as one of the more popular programming languages out there can be linked to the fact that it's relatively easy to learn and it allows users to accomplish several tasks using just a few lines of code.

Though this book wasn't designed to teach readers either the mechanics of programming or the implementation of machine learning algorithms, I have included plenty of helpful coding demonstrations and course recommendations over on this book's companion website (https://businessgrowth.ai). If you want to learn to get started with using Python to implement data science, you may want to check it out.

You can use Python to do anything, from simple mathematical operations to data visualizations and even machine learning and predictive analytics. Here's an example of a basic math operation in Python:

```
>>> 2.5+3
5.5
```

Figure 6-1 shows an example — taken from Python's Matplotlib library — of a more advanced output based on topographical data sets created by the National Oceanic and Atmospheric Administration (NOAA).

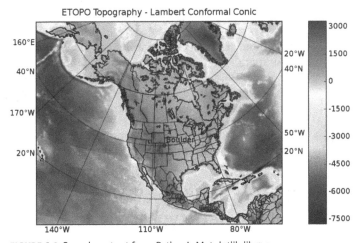

FIGURE 6-1: Sample output from Python's Matplotlib library.

Regardless of the task at hand, you should always study the most basic concepts of a language before trying to delve into its more specialized libraries. So, to start you off, keep in mind that, because Python is an object-oriented programming language, everything in Python is considered an object. In Python, an *object* is anything that can be assigned to a variable or passed as an argument to a function. The following items are all considered objects in the Python programming language:

>> Numbers

>> Strings

>> Lists

>> Tuples

>> Sets

>> Dictionaries

>> Functions

>> Classes

Additionally, all these items (except for the last two in the list) function as basic data types in plain ol' Python, which is Python with no external extensions added to it. (I introduce you to the external Python libraries NumPy, SciPy, pandas, Matplotlib, and scikit-learn in the later section "Checking out some useful Python libraries." When you add these libraries, additional data types become available to you.)

In Python, functions do basically the same thing as they do in plain math — they accept data inputs, process them, and output the result. Output results depend wholly on the task the function was programmed to do. Classes, on the other hand, are prototypes of objects that are designed to output additional objects.

REMEMBER

If your goal is to write fast, reusable, easy-to-modify code in Python, you must use functions and classes. Doing so helps to keep your code efficient and organized.

Sorting out the various Python data types

If you do much work with Python, you need to know how to work with different data types. Here are the main data types in Python and the general forms they take:

>> **Numbers:** Plain ol' numbers, obviously

>> **Strings:** ' . . . ' or " . . . "

- **Lists:** [. . . .] or [. . ., . . ., . . .]
- **Tuples:** (. . . .) or (. . ., . . ., . . .)
- **Sets:** Rarely used
- **Dictionaries:** {'Key': 'Value', . . .}

Numbers and strings are the most basic data types. You can incorporate them inside other, more complicated data types. All Python data types can be assigned to variables.

In Python, numbers, strings, lists, tuples, sets, and dictionaries are classified as both object types and data types.

REMEMBER

Numbers in Python

The *numbers* data type represents numeric values that you can use to handle all types of mathematical operations. Numbers come in the following types:

- **Integer:** A whole-number format
- **Long:** A whole-number format with an unlimited digit size
- **Float:** A real-number format, written with a decimal point
- **Complex:** An imaginary-number format, represented by the square root of –1

Strings in Python

Strings are the most often used data type in Python — and in every other programming language, for that matter. Simply put, a *string* consists of one or more characters written inside single or double quotes. The following code represents a string:

```
>>> variable1='This is a sample string'
>>> print(variable1)
This is a sample string
```

In this code snippet, the string is assigned to a variable and the variable subsequently acts like a storage container for the string value.

To print the characters contained inside the variable, simply use the predefined print function.

TIP

Python coders often refer to lists, tuples, sets, and dictionaries as data *structures* rather than data *types*. *Data structures* are basic functional units that organize data so that it can be used efficiently by the program or application you're working with.

REMEMBER

Lists, tuples, sets, and dictionaries are data structures, but keep in mind that they're still composed of one or more basic data types (numbers and/or strings, for example).

Lists in Python

A *list* is a sequence of numbers and/or strings. To create a list, you simply enclose the elements of the list (separated by commas) within square brackets. Here's an example of a basic list:

```
>>> variable2=["ID","Name","Depth","Latitude",
    "Longitude"]
>>> depth=[0,120,140,0,150,80,0,10]
>>> variable2[3]
'Latitude'
```

Every element of the list is automatically assigned an index number, starting from 0. You can access each element using this index, and the corresponding value of the list is returned. If you need to store and analyze long arrays of data, use lists — storing your data inside a list makes it fairly easy to extract statistical information. The following code snippet is an example of a simple computation to pull the mean value from the elements of the depth list created in the preceding code example:

```
>>> sum(depth)/len(depth)
62.5
```

In this example, the average of the list elements is computed by first summing up the elements, via the sum function, and then dividing them by the number of the elements contained in the list — a number you determine with the help of the len function, which returns the *length* (the number of elements, in other words) in a string, an array, or a list. The len function in the denominator here is what's returning the average value of items in the object. See? it's as simple as 1-2-3!

Tuples in Python

Tuples are just like lists, except that you can't modify their content after you create them. Also, to create tuples, you need to use normal brackets instead of squared ones.

"Normal brackets" refers to parentheses in the form of (. . .) or (. . ., . . ., . . .).

Here's an example of a tuple:

```
>>> depth=(0,120,140,0,150,80,0,10)
```

In this case, you can't modify any of the elements, as you would with a list. To ensure that your data stays in a read-only format, use tuples.

Sets in Python

A *set* is another data structure that's similar to a list. In contrast to lists, however, elements of a *set* are unordered. This disordered characteristic of a set makes it impossible to index, so it's not a commonly used data type.

Dictionaries in Python

Dictionaries are data structures that consist of pairs of keys and values. In a dictionary, every value corresponds to a certain key, and consequently, each value can be accessed using that key. The following code snippet shows a typical key/value pairing:

```
>>> variable4={"ID":1,"Name":"Valley City",
        "Depth":0,"Latitude":49.6,
        "Longitude":-98.01}
>>> variable4["Longitude"]
-98.01
```

Putting loops to good use in Python

When working with lists in Python, you typically access a list element by using the element index number. In a similar manner, you can access other elements of the list by using their corresponding index numbers. The following code snippet illustrates this concept:

```
>>>variable2=["ID","Name","Depth","Latitude",
    "Longitude"]
>>> print(variable2[3])
Latitude
>>> print(variable2[4])
Longitude
```

WARNING

Don't let the index numbering system confuse you. Every element of the list is automatically assigned an index number starting from 0 — *not* starting from 1. That means the fourth element in an index actually bears the index number 3.

When you're analyzing considerable amounts of data and you need to access each element of a list, this technique becomes quite inefficient. In these cases, you should use a looping technique instead.

You can use *looping* to execute the same block of code multiple times for a sequence of items. Consequently, instead of manually accessing all elements one by one, you simply create a loop to automatically *iterate* (pass through in successive cycles) each element of the list.

You can use two types of loops in Python: the for loop and the while loop. The most often used looping technique is the for loop — designed especially to iterate through sequences, strings, tuples, sets, and dictionaries. The following code snippet illustrates a for loop iterating through the variable2 list created in the preceding code snippet:

```
>>> for element in variable2:print(element)
ID
Name
Depth
Latitude
Longitude
```

The other available looping technique in Python is the while loop. Use a while loop to perform actions while a given condition is true.

REMEMBER

Looping is crucial when you work with long arrays of data, such as when you're working with raster images. Looping lets you apply certain actions to all data or apply those actions to only predefined groups of data.

Having fun with functions

Functions (and classes, which I describe in the following section) are the crucial building blocks of almost every programming language. They provide a way to build organized, reusable code. *Functions* are blocks of code that take an input, process it, and return an output. Function inputs can be numbers, strings, lists, objects, or other functions. Python has two types of functions: built-in and custom.

Built-in functions are predefined inside Python. You can use them by just typing their names. The following code snippet is an example of the built-in print function:

```
>>> print("Hello")
Hello
```

This oft-used, built-in print function prints a given input. The code behind print has already been written by the people who created Python. Now that this code stands in the background, you don't need to know how to code it yourself — you simply call the print function. The people who created the Python library couldn't guess every possible function to satisfy everyone's needs, but they managed to provide users with a way to create and reuse their own functions when necessary.

In the section "Sorting out the various Python data types," earlier in this chapter, the following code snippet from that section (listed again here) was used to sum up the elements in a list and calculate the average:

```
>>> depth=[0,120,140,0,150,80,0,10]
>>> sum(depth)/len(depth)
62.5
```

The preceding data represents snowfall and snow depth records from multiple point locations. As you can see, the points where snow depth measurements were collected have an average depth of 62.5 units. These are depth measurements taken at only one time, though. In other words, all the data bears the same time stamp. When modeling data using Python, you often see scenarios in which sets of measurements were taken at different times — known as *time series data.*

Here's an example of time series data:

```
>>> december_depth=[0,120,140,0,150,80,0,10]
>>> january_depth=[20,180,140,0,170,170,30,30]
>>> february_depth=[0,100,100,40,100,160,40,40]
```

You could calculate December, January, and February average snow depth in the same way you averaged values in the previous list, but that would be cumbersome. This is where custom functions come in handy:

```
>>> def average(any_list):return(sum(any_list)/
        len(any_list))
```

This code snippet defines the average function, which takes any list as input and calculates the average of its elements. The function isn't executed yet, but the code defines what the function does when it later receives some input values. In this snippet, any_list is just a variable that's later assigned the given value when the function is executed. To execute the function, all you need to do is pass it a value. In this case, the value is a real list with numerical elements:

```
>>> average(february_depth)
72.5
```

Executing a function is straightforward. You can use functions to do the same thing repeatedly, as many times as you need, for different input values. The beauty here is that, after the functions are constructed, you can reuse them without having to rewrite the calculating algorithm.

Keeping cool with classes

Classes are blocks of code that put together functions and variables to produce other objects. As such, they're slightly different from functions, which take an input and produce an output. The set of functions and classes tied together inside a class describes the blueprint of a certain object. In other words, classes spell out what has to happen in order for an object to be created. After you come up with a class, you can generate the actual object instance by calling a class instance. In Python, this is referred to as *instantiating* an object (creating an instance of that class).

Functions that are created inside a class are called *methods,* and variables within a class are called *attributes.* Methods describe the actions that generate the object, and attributes describe the actual object properties.

To better understand how to use classes for more efficient data analysis, consider the following scenario: Imagine that you have snow depth data from different locations and times and you're storing it online on an FTP server. The dataset contains different ranges of snow depth data, depending on the month of the year. Now imagine that every monthly range is stored in a different location on the FTP server.

Your task is to use Python to fetch all monthly data and then analyze the entire dataset, so you need to use different operations on the data ranges. First, you need to download the data from within Python by using an FTP handling library, such as ftplib. Then, to be able to analyze the data in Python, you need to store it in proper Python data types (in lists, tuples, or dictionaries, for example). After you fetch the data and store it as recognizable data types in a Python script, you can then apply more advanced operations that are available from specialized libraries such as NumPy, SciPy, pandas, Matplotlib, and scikit-learn.

In this scenario, you would want to create a class that creates a list containing the snow depth data for each month. Every monthly list would be an object instance generated by the class. The class itself would tie together the FTP downloading functions and the functions that store the downloaded records inside the lists. You could then instantiate the class for as many months as you need in order to carry out a thorough analysis. Here's the code to do something like this:

```
import ftplib

class Download:
    def __init__(self,site,dir,ftp=None,fileList
```

```
    =[]):
        self.ftp =ftp
        self.site=site
        self.dir=dir
        self.fileList=fileList
        self.login_ftp()
        self.fileList = self.store_in_list()
    def Login_ftp(self):
        self.ftp=ftplib.FTP(self.site)
        self.ftp.login()
    def store_in_list(self):
        self.fileList = []
        self.ftp.cwd("/")
        self.ftp.cwd(self.dir)
        self.ftp.retrlines('NLST',
            self.fileList.append)
        return self.fileList
```

Defining a class probably looks intimidating right now, but I simply want to give you a feeling for the basic structure and point out the class methods involved.

Delving into the preceding code, the keyword class defines the class, and the keyword def defines the class methods. The init function is a default function that you should always define when creating classes, because you use it to declare class variables. The login_ftp method is a custom function that you define to log in to the FTP server. After you log in using the login_ftp method and set the required directory where the data tables are located, you then store the data in a Python list using the custom function store_in_list.

After you finish defining the class, you can use it to produce objects. You just need to instantiate the class:

```
>>> Download("ftpexample.com","ftpdirectory")
```

And that's it! With this brief snippet, you've just declared the particular FTP domain and the internal FTP directory where the data is located. After you execute this last line, a list appears, giving you data that you can manipulate and analyze as needed.

Checking out some useful Python libraries

In Python, a *library* is a specialized collection of scripts that were written by someone else to perform specialized sets of tasks. To use specialized libraries in Python, you must first complete the installation process. After you install your libraries on your local hard drive, you can import any library's function into a project simply by using the import statement. For example, if you want to import the ftplib library, you write

```
>>> import ftplib
```

Be sure to import the library into your Python project before attempting to call its functions in your code.

After you import the library, you can use its functionality inside any of your scripts. Simply use *dot notation* (a shorthand way of accessing modules, functions, and classes in one line of code) to access the library. Here's an example of dot notation:

```
>>> ftplib.any_ftp_lib_function
```

The dot notation you see here tells the computer to open the "any_ftp_lib_function" that is found in the ftplib library.

Though you can choose from countless libraries to accomplish different tasks in Python, the Python libraries most commonly used in data science are Matplotlib, NumPy, pandas, scikit-learn, and SciPy. The NumPy and SciPy libraries were specially designed for scientific uses, pandas was designed for optimal data analysis performance, and Matplotlib was designed for data visualization. scikit-learn is Python's premiere machine learning library.

Saying hello to the NumPy library

NumPy (https://numpy.org) is the Python package that primarily focuses on working with *n*-dimensional array objects, and SciPy, described next, extends the capabilities of the NumPy library. When working with plain Python (Python with no external extensions, such as libraries, added to it), you're confined to storing your data in one-dimensional lists. If you extend Python by using the NumPy library, however, you're provided a basis from which you can work with *n*-dimensional arrays. (Just in case you were wondering, *n-dimensional* arrays are arrays of one dimension or of multiple dimensions.)

To enable NumPy in Python, you must first install and import the NumPy library. After that, you can generate multidimensional arrays.

To see how generating *n*-dimensional arrays works in practice, start by checking out the following code snippet, which shows how you'd create a one-dimensional NumPy array:

```
import numpy
>>> array_1d=numpy.arange(8)
>>> print(array_1d)
[0 1 2 3 4 5 6 7]
```

The `numpy.arange` method returns evenly spaced values from within a user specified interval. If you don't specify a number for `numpy.arange` to start with, it starts with 0. In this case, I specified that I want eight values, so numpy.arange returns [0 1 2 3 4 5 6 7].

After importing `numpy`, you can use it to generate *n*-dimensional arrays, such as the one-dimensional array just shown. One-dimensional arrays are referred to as *vectors*. You can also create multidimensional arrays using the `reshape` method, like this:

```
>>> array_2d=numpy.arange(8).reshape(2,4)
>>> print(array_2d)
[[0 1 2 3]
 [4 5 6 7]]
```

The preceding example is a two-dimensional array, otherwise known as a *2 x 4 matrix*. The only difference between this and the preceding example is that I called the `.reshape` method, and passed in a 2 and a 4 value — telling `numpy` to take the array and transform it into a 2 x 4 matrix.

Standard matrix notation is $m \times n$, where m is the number of rows and n specifies the number of columns in the matrix.

Using the `.arange` and `reshape` method is just one way to create NumPy arrays. You can also generate arrays from lists and tuples.

In the snow dataset that I introduce in the earlier section "Having fun with functions," I store my snow depth data for different locations inside three separate Python lists — one list per month:

```
>>> december_depth=[0,120,140,0,150,80,0,10]
>>> january_depth=[20,180,140,0,170,170,30,30]
>>> february_depth=[0,100,100,40,100,160,40,40]
```

It would be more efficient to have the measurements stored in a better-consolidated structure. For example, you can easily put all those lists in a single NumPy array by using the following code snippet:

```
>>>depth=numpy.array([december_depth,
        january_depth,february_depth])
>>> print(depth)
[[  0 120 140   0 150  80   0  10]
 [ 20 180 140   0 170 170  30  30]
 [  0 100 100  40 100 160  40  40]]
```

Using this structure allows you to pull out certain measurements more efficiently. For example, if you wanted to calculate the average of the snow depth for the first location in each of the three months, you'd extract the first elements of each horizontal row (values 0, 20, and 0, to be more precise). You can complete the extraction in a single line of code by taking a slice of the dataset and then calculating the mean by way of the NumPy mean function. The term *slicing* refers to taking a slice out of dataset. Here's an example:

```
>>> numpy.mean(depth[:,1])
133.33333333333334
```

With this code, I've instructed the computer to go to column index position 1 and calculate the mean of the value in that column. The values in the column at column index 1 are 120, 180, and 100. When you calculate the mean value of the numbers, you get 133.3.

Beyond using NumPy to extract information from single matrices, you can use it to interact with different matrices as well — applying standard mathematical operations between matrices, for example, or even applying nonstandard operators, such as matrix inversion, summarize, and minimum/maximum operators.

Array objects have the same rights as any other objects in Python. You can pass them as parameters to functions, set them as class attributes, or iterate through array elements to generate random numbers.

Getting up close and personal with the SciPy library

SciPy (https://scipy.org) is a collection of mathematical algorithms and sophisticated functions that extends the capabilities of the NumPy library. The SciPy library adds some specialized scientific functions to Python for more specific tasks in data science. To use SciPy's functions within Python, you must first install and import the SciPy library.

SciPy offers functionalities and algorithms for a variety of tasks, including vector quantization, statistical functions, discrete Fourier transform algorithms, orthogonal distance regression, airy functions, sparse eigenvalue solvers, maximum entropy fitting routines, n-dimensional image operations, integration routines, interpolation tools, sparse linear algebra, linear solvers, optimization tools, signal-processing tools, sparse matrices, and other utilities that aren't served by other Python libraries. Impressive, right? Yet that's not even a complete listing of the available SciPy utilities. If you're dying to get hold of a complete list, running the following code snippet in Python opens an extensive help module that explains the SciPy library:

```
>>> import scipy
>>> help(scipy)
```

You need to first download and install the SciPy library before you can use this code.

The help function used in the preceding code snippet returns a script that lists all utilities that comprise SciPy and documents all of SciPy's functions and classes. This information helps you understand what's behind the prewritten functions and algorithms that make up the SciPy library.

Because SciPy is still under development and, therefore, changing and growing, regularly check the help function to see what's changed.

Peeking into the pandas offering

The pandas library (https://pandas.pydata.org) makes data analysis much faster and easier with its accessible and robust data structures. Its precise purpose is to improve Python's performance with respect to data analysis and modeling. It even offers some data visualization functionality by integrating small portions of the Matplotlib library. Here are the two main pandas data structures:

>> Series: A Series object is an array-like structure that can assume either a horizontal or vertical dimension. You can think of a pandas Series object as being similar to one row or one column from a Microsoft Excel spreadsheet.

>> DataFrame: A DataFrame object acts like a tabular data table in Python. Each row or column in a DataFrame can be accessed and treated as its own pandas Series object.

Indexing is integrated into both data structure types, making it easy to access and manipulate your data. pandas offers functionality for reading in and writing out your data, which makes it easy to use for loading, transferring, and saving datasets in whatever formats you want. Lastly, pandas offers excellent functionality for reshaping data, treating missing values, and removing outliers, among other tasks. This makes pandas an excellent choice for data preparation and basic data analysis tasks. If you want to carry out more advanced statistical and machine learning methods, you'll need to use the scikit-learn library. The good news is that scikit-learn and pandas play well together.

Bonding with Matplotlib for data visualization

Generally speaking, data science projects usually culminate in visual representations of objects or phenomena. In Python, things are no different. After taking baby steps (or some not-so-baby steps) with NumPy and SciPy, you can use Python's Matplotlib library (https://matplotlib.org) to create complex visual representations of your dataset or data analysis findings. Matplotlib, when combined with NumPy and SciPy, creates an excellent environment in which to work when solving problems using data science.

Looking more closely at Matplotlib, I can tell you that it's a two-dimensional plotting library you can use in Python to produce figures from data. You can use Matplotlib to produce plots, histograms, scatterplots, and a variety of other data graphics. What's more, because the library gives you full control of your visualization's symbology, line styles, fonts, and colors, you can even use Matplotlib to produce publication-quality data graphics.

As is the case with all other libraries in Python, in order to work with Matplotlib, you first need to install and import the library into your script. After you complete those tasks, it's easy to get started producing graphs and charts.

To illustrate how to use Matplotlib, consider the following NumPy array (which I came up with in the "Saying hello to the NumPy library" section, earlier in this chapter):

```
>>> print(depth)
[[  0 120 140   0 150  80   0  10]
 [ 20 180 140   0 170 170  30  30]
 [  0 100 100  40 100 160  40  40]]
```

With the following few lines of code, using just a for loop and a Matplotlib function — pyplot — you can easily plot all measurements in a single graph within Python:

```
>>> import matplotlib.pyplot as plt
>>> for month in depth:
    plt.plot(month)
>>> plt.show()
```

This code snippet instantly generates the line chart you see in Figure 6-2.

Each line in the graph represents the depth of snow at different locations in the same month. The preceding code you use to build this graph is simple; if you want to make a better representation, you can add color or text font attributes to the plot function. Of course, you can also use other types of data graphics, depending on which types best show the data trends you want to display. What's important here is that you know when to use each of these important libraries and that you understand how you can use the Python programming language to make data analysis both easy and efficient.

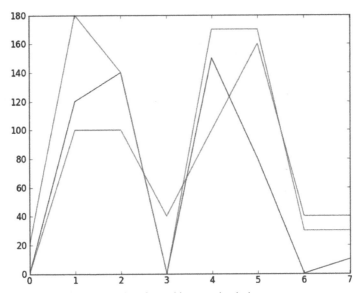

FIGURE 6-2: Time series plot of monthly snow depth data.

Learning from data with scikit-learn

scikit-learn (`https://scikit-learn.org`) is far and away Python's best machine learning library. With it, you can execute all sorts of machine learning methods, including classification, regression, clustering, dimensionality reduction, and more. The library also offers a preprocessing module that is wonderfully supportive whenever you need to prepare your data for predictive modeling. Lastly, scikit-learn offers a model selection module that's readily available with all sorts of metrics to help you build your models and choose the best-performing model among a selection.

Chapter **7**

Generating Insights with Software Applications

I n this day and age, when it seems that every company wants to hire data scientists with extensive experience programming in R and Python, it only makes sense for technology vendors to offer tools that help democratize the data insights that are generated by data scientists. There simply aren't enough data scientists to go around, and even if there were, the whole world doesn't need to be a data scientist. We need to be able to show up and create value in our own areas of expertise. The business world needs that from us as well.

In this chapter, you see some incredibly powerful low-code or no-code tools for generating more profits, faster, from the data you're already working with, without the downtime of needing to learn to build complicated predictive models in R or Python.

Choosing the Best Tools for Your Data Science Strategy

Data science strategy can best be described as a technical plan that maps out each and every element required to lead data science projects that increase the profitability of a business. In Chapter 6, I talk about how Python is often part of the plan, which may make you think that, when it comes to data science strategy, Python is the obvious answer to this question: "Which tools do I need for my strategy to succeed?" Is the obvious answer always the best answer? I think not. A data strategy that relies *only* on data science to improve profits from data is a limited one, cutting itself off at the pass by insisting on the use of code to monetize data.

In recent years, no-code and low-code platforms have seen significant advancements. They've incorporated more artificial intelligence (AI) and machine learning (ML) capabilities to further streamline data processing and automation. By making it relatively straightforward for users to build sophisticated applications without writing code, platforms like Google AppSheet, Make, and Airtable AI have positioned themselves at the forefront of this revolution. These tools make it simple to build data-driven applications that integrate seamlessly with popular cloud services (like Amazon Web Services [AWS], Google Cloud, and Microsoft Azure) and generative AI (GenAI) services (like OpenAI and Hugging Face). As a result, these tools are powerful solutions for both advanced analytics and AI automation.

For example, imagine that a human resources (HR) professional, without needing to write even one line of code, is able to build a software application that automatically collects applicant data, reads that data into an applicants Structured Query Language (SQL) database, and then executes an automated response to each applicant based on the manual determination of the HR personnel who is processing employment applications. Where appropriate, the software automatically moves candidates forward in the hiring process. This no-code application eliminates the need for manual data entry, data cleanup, email follow-up, and candidate forwarding. That's a lot of time (money, in other words) saved right there.

Do you know of any prebuilt software whose vendor could come in and configure it to create this type of system setup in-house? Yes, you probably do, but that's a lengthy, expensive, and inflexible route to take, considering that the same outcome is now possible within modern no-code environments like Airtable — environments that are designed to act and work like both a spreadsheet and a database simultaneously, and that provide a collaborative, intuitive, cloud-based SQL-esque solution. In my business, all our data warehousing and project management takes place inside Airtable, where we can build applications while collaborating between team members, all for a minimal cost. By leveraging AI-driven features and seamless cloud integration, these platforms enable rapid development and deployment of data applications, in turn democratizing data insights and empowering knowledge workers to generate more value without extensive technical expertise.

No-code is a type of development platform that leverages graphical user interfaces (GUIs) in a way that allows both coders and noncoders alike to build their own software applications. If your start-up or small business has no complex data architecture, it's entirely possible to house your company's data in a no-code environment and not have to worry about integrating that data and platform with other data systems you may have.

If your company is larger and more mature, you may want to look into *low-code* options — platforms that allow users to build applications without needing to use any code whatsoever, but that require a small bit of code to configure on the back end in order to enable data integration with the rest of the company's data systems and sources. Commonly used low-code solutions are Microsoft Power Platform (for application development, automation, and analytics), as well as Google Forms and Microsoft Access for self-service data collection and integration.

With respect to data strategy, what we're really talking about here is leveraging low-code and no-code solutions to deploy and directly monetize more of your company's data, without needing to train existing team members or hire experienced data scientists. The idea is to equip all knowledge workers with intuitive data technologies they can use right away to start getting better results from data themselves, without the intervention of data specialists — a true democratization of data and data monetization across the business, in other words.

Bridging the gap between no-code, low-code, SQL, and spreadsheets, SQL databases and spreadsheet applications such as Excel and Google Sheets provide just the no-code and low-code environments that knowledge workers can start using today to increase the productivity and profitability of their company's data. These technologies are so accessible and represent so much upside potential to modern businesses that I include high-level coverage of them in the pages that follow.

Getting a Handle on SQL and Relational Databases

Some data professionals are resistant to learning SQL because of the steep learning curve involved. They think, "I'm not a coder, and Structured Query Language sure *sounds* like a programming language to me." In the case of SQL, though, it's *not* a programming language, as you'll soon see. As far as the upside potential goes of learning to use SQL to query and access data, it's worth the small degree of hassle.

SQL is a standard for creating, maintaining, and securing relational databases. It's a set of rules you can use to quickly and efficiently query, update, modify, add, or remove data from large and complex databases. You use SQL rather than Python or a spreadsheet application to do these tasks because SQL is the simplest, fastest way to get the job done. It offers a plain and standardized set of core commands and methods that are easy to use when performing these particular tasks. In this chapter, I introduce you to basic SQL concepts and explain how you can use SQL to do cool things like query, join, group, sort, and even text-mine structured datasets.

REMEMBER

Although the SQL standard is lengthy, a user commonly needs fewer than 20 commands, and the syntax is human-readable — for example, if you need to pull data on employees in the finance department who earn more than $50,000 per year in salary, you could use an SQL statement like the one shown in Figure 7-1. Making things even easier, SQL commands are written in all caps, which helps to keep the language distinct and separate in your mind from other programming languages.

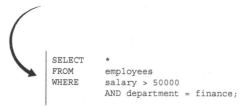

```
SELECT*FROM employees WHERE salary>50000 AND department=finance;


SELECT      *
FROM        employees
WHERE       salary > 50000
            AND department = finance;
```

FIGURE 7-1: An example of how SQL is human-readable.

Although you can use SQL to work with structured data that resides in relational database management systems, you can't use standard SQL as a solution for unstructured or semistructured data. I give you more solutions for handling these types of data in Chapter 2, where I discuss data engineering and its components. For now, suffice it to say that SQL is simply a tool you can use to manipulate and edit structured data tables. It's nothing exceedingly innovative, but it can be helpful to use SQL for the data querying and manipulation tasks that often arise in the practice of data science. In this chapter, I introduce the basics of relational databases, SQL, and database design.

REMEMBER

Although the name Structured Query Language suggests that SQL is a programming language, don't be misled. SQL is not a programming language, like R or Python. Instead, it's a language of commands and syntax that you can use to create, maintain, and search relational database systems. SQL supports a few common programming forms, like conditionals and loops, but to do anything more complex, you'd have to import your SQL query results into another programming platform and then do the more complex work there.

One fundamental characteristic of SQL is that you can use it on only structured data that sits in a relational database. SQL database management systems (DBMSs) optimize their own structure with minimal user input, which enables blazing-fast operational performance.

REMEMBER

An *index* is the lookup table. You create it in order to index, point to, and "look up" data in tables of a database. Although SQL DBMSs are known for their fast structured database querying capabilities, this speed and effectiveness are heavily dependent on good indexing. Good indexing is vital for fast data retrieval in SQL.

Similar to how different web browsers comply with, add to, and ignore different parts of the HTML standard in different ways, SQL rules are interpreted a bit differently, depending on whether you're working with open-source products or commercial vendor software applications. Because not every SQL solution is the same, it's a good idea to know something about the benefits and drawbacks of some of the more popular SQL solutions on the market. Here are two popular open-source SQL implementations commonly used by data scientists:

>> **MySQL:** By far the most popular open-source version of SQL, MySQL offers a complete and powerful version of SQL. It's used on the back end of millions of websites.

>> **PostgreSQL:** This software adds object-oriented elements to SQL's relational language, making it popular with programmers who want to integrate SQL objects into their own platforms' object model.

REMEMBER

Other powerful commercial SQL implementations, such as Oracle and Microsoft SQL Server, are great solutions as well, but they're designed for use in a more traditional business context rather than as a data science tool.

As you may guess from the name, the most salient aspect of relational databases is that they're *relational* — they're composed of related tables. To illustrate the idea of a relational database, first imagine an Excel spreadsheet with rows, columns, and predefined relationships between shared columns. Then imagine having an Excel workbook with many worksheets (tables), in which every worksheet has a column with the same name as a column in one or more *other* worksheets. Because these worksheets have a shared relationship, if you use SQL you can use that shared relationship to look up data in all related worksheets. This type of relationship is illustrated in Figure 7-2.

REMEMBER

The *primary key* of a table is a column of values that uniquely identifies every row in that table. A good example of primary keys is the use of ISBNs for a table of books or employee ID numbers for a table of employees. A *foreign key* is a column in one table that matches the primary key of another and is used to link tables.

Foreign Key		
Lake Name	Max Water Depth (ft)	Average Annual Depth Change (in)
Lake Monroe	...	...
Lake Lilly	...	...
Lake Conway	...	...

Primary Key

Lake Name	Alkalinity (mEq/L)	Total Dissolved Solids (ppm)	Phosphates (u g/L)
Lake Monroe	...	...	...
Lake Lilly	...	...	...
Lake Conway	...	...	...

Foreign Key

Lake Name	Subdivision Name	Taxing District
Lake Monroe	...	...
Lake Lilly	...	...
Lake Conway	...	...

FIGURE 7-2: A relationship between data tables that share a column.

Keeping the focus on terminology, remember that proper database science often associates particular meanings to particular words, as you can see in this list:

>> **Columns,** called *fields, keys,* and *attributes*

>> **Rows,** called *records*

>> **Cells,** called *values*

Database science uses a *lot* of synonyms. For simplicity's sake, I try to stick to using the words *column, row,* and *cell.* And because *primary key* and *foreign key* are standard terms, I use them to describe these two special column types.

The main benefits of using relational database management systems (RDBMSs) is that they're fast, they have large storage and handling capacity (compared to spreadsheet applications such as Excel), and they're ideal tools to help you maintain *data integrity* (the consistency and accuracy of data in your database). If you need to make quick and accurate changes and updates to your datasets, you can use SQL and an RDBMS.

Let the following scenario serve as an illustration. This data table describes films and lists ratings from viewers:

```
id    title          genre    rating timestamp      rating
1     The Even Couple  NULL    2011-08-03 16:04:23    4
```

```
2    The Fourth Man    Drama      2014-02-19 19:17:16   5
2    The Fourth Man    Drama      2010-04-27 10:05:36   4
3    All About Adam    Drama      2011-04-05 21:21:05   4
3    All About Adam    Drama      2014-02-21 00:11:07   3
4    Dr. Yes           Thriller   NULL
```

What happens if you find out that *All About Adam* is a comedy rather than a drama? If the table were in a simple spreadsheet, you'd have to open the data table, find all instances of the film, and then manually change the genre value for that record. That's not so difficult in this sample table because only two records are related to that film. But even here, if you forget to change one of these records, this inconsistency would cause a loss of data integrity, which can cause all sorts of unpredictable problems for you down the road.

In contrast, the relational database solution is simple and elegant. Instead of one table for this example, you'd have three:

```
Film    id    title
        1     The Even Couple
        2     The Fourth Man
        3     All About Adam
        4     Dr. Yes



Genre   id    genre
        2     Drama
        3     Drama
        4     Thriller


Rating  timestamp              id    rating
        2011-08-03 16:04:23    1     4
        2014-02-19 19:17:16    2     5
        2010-04-27 10:05:36    2     4
        2011-04-05 21:21:05    3     4
        2014-02-21 00:11:07    3     3
```

The primary key for the Film and Genre tables is id. The primary key for the Rating table is timestamp — because a film can have more than one rating, id is not a unique field, so it can't be used as a primary key. In this example, if you want to look up and change the genre for *All About Adam*, you'd use Film.id as the primary key and `Genre.id` as the foreign key. You'd simply use these keys to query the records you need to change and then apply the changes systematically. This systematic approach eliminates the risk of stray errors.

Investing Some Effort into Database Design

If you want to ensure that your database will be useful to you for the foreseeable future, you need to invest time and resources into excellent database design. If you want to create databases that offer fast performance and error-free results, your database design has to be flawless — or as flawless as you can manage. Before you enter any data into a data table, first carefully consider the tables and columns you want to include, the kinds of data those tables will hold, and the relationships you want to create between those tables.

REMEMBER

Every hour you spend planning your database and anticipating future needs can save you countless hours down the road, when your database may hold a million records. Poorly planned databases can easily turn into slow, error-ridden monstrosities — avoid them at all costs.

Keep just a few concepts in mind when you design databases:

>> Data types
>> Constraints
>> Normalization

In the next few sections, I offer a closer look at each topic.

Defining data types

When creating a data table, one of the first things you have to do is define the data type of each column. You have several data type options to choose from:

>> **Text:** If your column is to contain text values, you can classify it as a Character data type with a fixed length or a Text data type of indeterminate length.

>> **Numerical:** If your column is to hold number values, you can classify it as a Numerical data type. Numerical data types can be stored as integers or floats.

>> **Date:** If your column is to hold date- or time-based values, you can designate this as a Date data type or Date-Time data type.

REMEMBER

Text data types are handy, but they're terrible for searches. When you use a text field to do a search or select query, SQL will cause the computer to call up each of the data objects individually, instead of searching and sorting through them *in-memory* — in other words, processing data within the computer's memory, without actually reading and writing its computational results onto the disk.

Designing constraints properly

Think of constraints, in the context of SQL, as rules you use to control the type of data that can be placed in a table. As such, they're an important consideration in any database design. When you're considering adding constraints, first decide whether each column is allowed to hold a NULL value. (NULL isn't the same as blank or zero data; it indicates a total absence of data in a cell.)

For example, if you have a table of products you're selling, you probably don't want to allow a NULL in the Price column. In the Product Description column, however, some products may have *long* descriptions, so you may allow some of the cells in this column to contain NULL values.

Within any data type, you can also constrain exactly what type of input values the column accepts. Imagine that you have a text field for Employee ID, which must contain values that are exactly two letters followed by seven numbers, like this: SD0154919. Because you don't want your database to accept a typo, you'd define a constraint that requires all values entered into the cells of the Employee ID column to have exactly two letters followed by seven numbers.

Normalizing your database

After you've defined the data types and designed constraints, you need to deal with *normalization* (structuring your database so that any changes, additions, or deletions to the data have to be made only once and won't result in anomalous, inconsistent data). There are many different degrees and types of normalization (at least seven), but a good, robust, normalized SQL database should have at least the following properties:

>> **Primary keys:** Each table has a primary key, which is a unique value for every row in that column.

>> **Nonredundancy of columns:** No two tables have the same column, unless it's the primary key of one and the foreign key of the other.

>> **No multiple dependencies:** Every column's value must depend on only one other column whose value does not, in turn, depend on any other column. Calculated values — values such as the total for an invoice, for example — must, therefore, be done on the fly for each query and should not be hard-coded into the database. This means that zip codes should be stored in a separate table because they depend on three columns — address, city, and state.

>> **Column indexes:** As you may recall, in SQL an index is a lookup table that points to data in tables of a database. When you make a column index — an index of a particular column — each record in that column is assigned a unique key value that's indexed in a lookup table. Column indexing enables faster data retrieval from that column.

Creating a column index for frequent searches or to be used as a search criterion is an excellent idea. The column index takes up memory, but it increases your search speeds tremendously. It's easy to set up, too. Just tell your SQL DBMS to index a certain column, and then the system sets it up for you.

TIP

If you're concerned that your queries are slow, first make sure that you have all the indexes you need before trying other, perhaps more involved, troubleshooting efforts.

>> **Subject-matter segregation:** Another feature of good database design is that each table contains data for only one kind of subject matter. This isn't exactly a normalization principle per se, but it helps to achieve a similar end.

Consider again the film rating example, from earlier in this chapter:

```
Film    id    title
        1     The Even Couple
        2     The Fourth Man
        3     All About Adam
        4     Dr. Yes




Genre   id    genre
        2     Drama
        3     Drama
        4     Thriller




Rating  timestamp              id    rating
        2011-08-03 16:04:23    1     4
        2014-02-19 19:17:16    2     5
        2010-04-27 10:05:36    2     4
        2011-04-05 21:21:05    3     4
        2014-02-21 00:11:07    3     3
```

- I could have designated Genre to be a separate column in the Film table, but it's better off in its own table because that allows for the possibility of missing data values (NULLs). Look at the Film table just shown. Film 1 has no genre assigned to it. If the Genre column were included in this table, then Film 1 would have a NULL value there. Rather than have a column that contains a NULL value, it's much easier to make a separate Genre data table. The primary keys of the Genre table don't align exactly with those of the Film table, but they don't need to when you go to join them.

TIP

NULL values can be quite problematic when you're running a SELECT query. When you're querying based on the value of particular attribute, any records that have a NULL value for that attribute won't be returned in the query results. Of course, these records would still exist, and they may even fall within the specified range of values you've defined for your query, but if the record has a NULL value, it's omitted from the query results. In this case, you're likely to miss them in your analysis.

Any data scientist worth their salt must address many challenges when dealing with either the data or the science. SQL takes some of the pressure off when you're dealing with the time-consuming tasks of storing and querying data, saving precious time and effort.

Narrowing the Focus with SQL Functions

When working with SQL commands, you use *functions* to perform tasks, and *arguments* to more narrowly specify those tasks. To query a particular set from within your data tables, for example, use the SELECT function. To combine separate tables into one, use the JOIN function. To place limits on the data that your query returns, use a WHERE argument. As I mention earlier in this chapter, fewer than 20 commands are commonly used in SQL. This section introduces SELECT, FROM, JOIN, WHERE, GROUP, MAX(), MIN(), COUNT(), AVG(), and HAVING.

The most common SQL command is SELECT. You can use this function to generate a list of search results based on designated criteria. To illustrate, imagine the film-rating scenario mentioned earlier in this chapter with a tiny database of movie ratings that contains the three tables Film, Genre, and Rating.

To generate a printout of all data FROM the Rating table, use the SELECT function. Any function with SELECT is called a *query*, and SELECT functions accept different arguments to narrow down or expand the data that is returned. An asterisk (*) represents a wildcard, so the asterisk in SELECT * tells the *interpreter* (the SQL component that carries out all SQL statements) to show every column in the table. You can then use the WHERE argument to limit the output to only certain values. For example, here is the complete Rating table:

Rating	timestamp	id	rating
	2011-08-03 16:04:23	1	4
	2014-02-19 19:17:16	2	5
	2010-04-27 10:05:36	2	4
	2011-04-05 21:21:05	3	4
	2014-02-21 00:11:07	3	3

If you want to limit your ratings to those made after a certain time, you'd use code like the following:

```
SELECT * FROM Rating
WHERE Rating.timestamp >= date('2014-01-01')
timestamp            id    rating
2014-02-19 19:17:16  2     5
2014-02-21 00:11:07  3     3
```

Here, the DATE() function turns a string into a date that can then be compared with the timestamp column.

You can also use SQL to join columns into a new data table. Joins are made on the basis of shared (or compared) data in a particular column (or columns). You can execute a join in SQL in several ways, but the ones listed here are probably the most popular:

>> **Inner join:** The default JOIN type; returns all records that lie in the intersecting regions between the tables being queried

>> **Outer join:** Returns all records that lie outside the overlapping regions between queried data tables

>> **Full outer join:** Returns all records that lie both inside and outside the overlapping regions between queried data tables — in other words, returns all records for both tables

>> **Left join:** Returns all records that reside in the leftmost table

>> **Right join:** Returns all records that reside in the rightmost table

REMEMBER

Be sure to differentiate between an inner join and an outer join, because these functions handle missing data in different ways. As an example of a join in SQL, if you want a list of films that includes genres, you use an inner join between the Film and Genre tables to return only the results that intersect (overlap) between the two tables.

To refresh your memory, here are the two tables you're interested in:

```
Film    id   title
        1    The Even Couple
        2    The Fourth Man
        3    All About Adam
        4    Dr. Yes


Genre   id   genre
        2    Drama
        3    Drama
        4    Thriller
```

Here's how you'd use an inner join to find the information you want:

```
SELECT Film.id, Film.title, Genre.genre
FROM Film
JOIN Genre On Genre.id=Film.id
id   title              genre
2    The Fourth Man     Drama
3    All About Adam     Drama
4    Dr. Yes            Thriller
```

Here, I name specific columns (Film.title and Genre.genre) after the SELECT command. I do this to avoid creating a duplicate id column in the table that results from the JOIN — one id from the Film table and one id from the Genre table. Because the default for JOIN is inner, and inner joins return only records that are overlapping or shared between tables, Film 1 is omitted from the results (because of its missing Genre value).

If you want to return all rows, even ones with NULL values, simply do a full outer join, like the one shown here:

```
SELECT Film.id, Film.title, Genre.genre
FROM Film
FULL JOIN Genre On Genre.id=Film.id
id   title              genre
```

```
1    The Even Couple    NULL
2    The Fourth Man     Drama
3    All About Adam     Drama
4    Dr. Yes            Thriller
```

To aggregate values so that you can figure out the average rating for a film, use the GROUP statement. (GROUP statement commands include MAX( ), MIN( ), COUNT( ), or AVG( ).)

The following code shows one way you can aggregate values in order to return the average rating of each film. The SELECT function uses the AS statement to rename the column to make sure it was properly labeled. The Film and Ratings tables had to be joined and, because *Dr. Yes* had no ratings and an inner join was used, that film was left out.

```
SELECT Film.title, AVG(rating) AS avg_rating
FROM Film
JOIN Rating On Film.id=Rating.id
GROUP BY Film.title


title            avg_rating
All About Adam   3.5
The Even Couple  4.0
The Fourth Man   4.5
```

To narrow the results even further, add a HAVING clause at the end, as shown here:

```
SELECT Film.title, AVG(rating) AS avg_rating
FROM Film
JOIN Rating On Film.id=Rating.id
GROUP BY Film.title
HAVING avg_rating >= 4


title            avg_rating
The Even Couple  4.0
The Fourth Man   4.5
```

This code limits the data your query returns so you get only records of titles that have an average rating greater than or equal to 4.

Making Life Easier with Excel

Microsoft Excel holds a special place among data science tools. It was originally designed to act as a simple spreadsheet. Over time, however, it has become the people's choice in data analysis software. In response to user demands, Microsoft has added more and more analysis and visualization tools with every release. As Excel advances, so do its data munging and data science capabilities. (*Data munging* involves reformatting and rearranging data into more manageable formats that are usually required for consumption by other processing applications downstream.) Excel includes easy-to-use tools for charting, PivotTables, and macros. It also supports scripting in Visual Basic so you can design scripts to automate repeatable tasks.

The benefit of using Excel in a data science capacity is that it offers a fast and easy way to get up close and personal with your data. If you want to browse every data point in your dataset, you can quickly and easily do this using Excel. Most data scientists start in Excel and eventually add other tools and platforms when they find themselves pushing against the boundaries of the tasks Excel is designed to do. Still, even the best data scientists out there keep Excel as an important tool in their tool belt. When working in data science, you may not use Excel every day, but knowing how to use it can make your job easier.

TIP

If you're using Excel spreadsheets for data analysis but finding it to be rather buggy and clunky, I recommend that you instead test out Google Sheets — Google's cloud-based version of a spreadsheet application. It can be run offline on your computer, and it offers an ease of use and a set of collaborative features that simply aren't available within the Microsoft Office environment today. Google Sheets offers all the same functions discussed in this chapter, using all the same commands as Excel spreadsheets, but most users find Sheets to be a far more intuitive, extensible tool for data analysis, visualization, and collaboration.

REMEMBER

Although you have many different tools available to you when you want to see your data as one big forest, Excel is a great first choice when you need to look at the trees. Excel attempts to be many different things to many different kinds of users. Its functionality is well compartmentalized in order to avoid overwhelming new users while still providing power users with the more advanced functionality they crave.

In the following sections, I show you how you can use Excel to quickly get to know your data. I also introduce Excel PivotTables and macros and tell you how you can use them to greatly simplify your data cleanup and analysis tasks.

Using Excel to quickly get to know your data

If you're just starting off with an unfamiliar dataset and you need to spot patterns or trends as quickly as possible, use Excel. Excel offers effective features for exactly these purposes. Its main features for a quick-and-dirty data analysis are

>> **Filters:** Filters are useful for sorting out all records that are irrelevant to the analysis at hand.

>> **Conditional formatting:** Specify a condition, and Excel flags records that meet that condition. By using conditional formatting, you can easily detect outliers and trends in your tabular datasets.

>> **Charts:** Charts have long been used to visually detect outliers and trends in data, so charting is an integral part of almost all data science analyses.

To see how these features work in action, consider the sample dataset shown in Figure 7-3, which tracks sales figures for three employees over six months.

Filtering in Excel

To narrow your view of your dataset to only the data that matters for your analysis, use Excel filters to filter out irrelevant data from the data view. Simply select the data and click the Home tab's Sort & Filter button; then choose Filter from the options that appear. A little drop-down option appears in the header row of the selected data so you can select the classes of records you want to have filtered from the selection. Using the Excel Filter functionality allows you to quickly and easily sort or restrict your view to only the subsets of the data that interest you the most.

Salesperson	Month	Total Sales
Abbie	Jan	$ 10,144.75
Abbie	Feb	$ 29,008.52
Abbie	Mar	$ 208,187.70
Abbie	Apr	$ 21,502.13
Abbie	May	$ 23,975.73
Abbie	Jun	$ 20,172.20
Brian	Jan	$ 9,925.44
Brian	Feb	$ 9,183.93
Brian	Mar	$ 12,691.39
Brian	Apr	$ 19,521.37
Brian	May	$ 16,579.38
Brian	Jun	$ 14,161.52
Chris	Jan	$ 2,792.18
Chris	Feb	$ 5,669.46
Chris	Mar	$ 4,909.24
Chris	Apr	$ 8,731.14
Chris	May	$ 11,747.29
Chris	Jun	$ 13,856.17

FIGURE 7-3: The full dataset that tracks employee sales performance.

Take another look at the full dataset shown in Figure 7-3. Say you want to view only data related to Abbie's sales figures. If you select all records in the Salesperson column and then activate the filter functionality (as just described), from the drop-down menu that appears you can specify that the filter should isolate only all records named Abbie, as shown in Figure 7-4. When filtered, the table is reduced from 18 rows to only 6 rows. In this particular example, that change doesn't seem so dramatic, but when you have hundreds, thousands, or even a million rows, this feature comes in very, very handy.

Salesperson	Month	Total Sales
Abbie	Jan	$10,144.75
Abbie	Feb	$29,008.52
Abbie	Mar	$208,187.70
Abbie	Apr	$21,502.13
Abbie	May	$23,975.73
Abbie	Jun	$20,172.20

FIGURE 7-4: The sales performance dataset, filtered to show only Abbie's records.

WARNING

Excel lets you store only up to 1,048,576 rows per worksheet.

Using conditional formatting

To quickly spot outliers in your tabular data, use Excel's Conditional Formatting feature. Imagine after a data entry error that Abbie's March total sales showed $208,187.70 but was supposed to be only $20,818.77. You're not quite sure where the error is located, but you know that it must be significant because the figures seem off by about $180,000.

To quickly show such an outlier, select all records in the Total Sales column and then click the Conditional Formatting button on the Ribbon's Home tab. When the button's menu appears, choose the Data Bars option. Doing so displays the red data bar scales shown in Figure 7-5. With data bars turned on, the bar in the $208,187.70 cell is so much larger than any of the others that you can easily see the error.

If you want to quickly discover patterns in your tabular data, you can choose the Color Scales option (rather than the Data Bars option) from the Conditional Formatting menu. After correcting Abbie's March Total Sales figure to $20,818.77, select all cells in the Total Sales column and then activate the Color Scales version of conditional formatting. Doing so displays the result shown in Figure 7-6. From the red-white-blue heat map, you can see that Abbie has the highest sales total and Brian has been selling more than Chris. (Okay, you can't see the red-white-blue in my black-and-white figures, but you can see the light-versus-dark contrast.) Now, if you only want to conditionally format Abbie's sales performance relative to her own total sales (but not Brian's and Chris's sales), you can select only the cells for Abbie (and not the entire column).

Salesperson	Month	Total Sales
Abbie	Jan	$ 10,144.75
Abbie	Feb	$ 29,008.52
Abbie	Mar	$ 208,187.70
Abbie	Apr	$ 21,502.13
Abbie	May	$ 23,975.73
Abbie	Jun	$ 20,172.20
Brian	Jan	$ 9,925.44
Brian	Feb	$ 9,183.93
Brian	Mar	$ 12,691.39
Brian	Apr	$ 19,521.37
Brian	May	$ 16,579.38
Brian	Jun	$ 14,161.52
Chris	Jan	$ 2,792.18
Chris	Feb	$ 5,669.46
Chris	Mar	$ 4,909.24
Chris	Apr	$ 8,731.14
Chris	May	$ 11,747.29
Chris	Jun	$ 13,856.17

FIGURE 7-5: Spotting outliers in a tabular dataset with conditional formatting data bars.

Excel charting to visually identify outliers and trends

Excel's Charting tool gives you an incredibly easy way to visually identify both outliers and trends in your data. An XY (scatter) chart of the original dataset (refer to Figure 7-3) yields the scatterplot shown in Figure 7-7. As you can see, the outlier is overwhelmingly obvious when the data is plotted on a scatter chart.

Alternatively, if you want to visually detect trends in a dataset, you can use Excel's Line Chart feature. The data from Figure 7-6 is shown as a line chart in Figure 7-8. It's worth mentioning, I've fixed the outlier in this line graph, which is what allows the y-axis to have a more readable scale compared to Figure 7-7.

As you can clearly see from the figure, Chris's sales performance is low — last place among the three salespeople but gaining momentum. Because Chris seems to be improving, maybe management will want to wait a few months before making any firing decisions based on sales performance data.

Salesperson	Month	Total Sales
Abbie	Jan	$ 10,144.75
Abbie	Feb	$ 29,008.52
Abbie	Mar	$ 20,818.77
Abbie	Apr	$ 21,502.13
Abbie	May	$ 23,975.73
Abbie	Jun	$ 20,172.20
Brian	Jan	$ 9,925.44
Brian	Feb	$ 9,183.93
Brian	Mar	$ 12,691.39
Brian	Apr	$ 19,521.37
Brian	May	$ 16,579.38
Brian	Jun	$ 14,161.52
Chris	Jan	$ 2,792.18
Chris	Feb	$ 5,669.46
Chris	Mar	$ 4,909.24
Chris	Apr	$ 8,731.14
Chris	May	$ 11,747.29
Chris	Jun	$ 13,856.17

FIGURE 7-6: Spotting outliers in a tabular dataset with color scales.

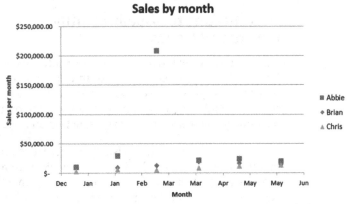

FIGURE 7-7: Excel XY (scatter) plots provide a simple way to visually detect outliers.

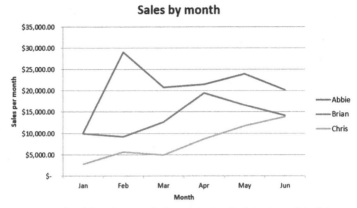

FIGURE 7-8: Excel line charts make it easy to visually detect trends in data.

Reformatting and summarizing with PivotTables

Excel developed the PivotTable to make it easier for users to extract valuable insights from large sets of spreadsheet data. If you want to generate insights by quickly restructuring or reclassifying your data, use a PivotChart. One of the main differences between a traditional spreadsheet and a dataset is that spreadsheets tend to be wide (with a lot of columns) and datasets tend to be long (with a lot of rows). Figure 7-9 clearly shows the difference between a long dataset and a wide spreadsheet.

Long format:

Salesperson	Month	Total Sales
Abbie	Jan	$ 10,144.75
Abbie	Feb	$ 29,008.52
Abbie	Mar	$ 208,187.70
Abbie	Apr	$ 21,502.13
Abbie	May	$ 23,975.73
Abbie	Jun	$ 20,172.20
Brian	Jan	$ 9,925.44
Brian	Feb	$ 9,183.93
Brian	Mar	$ 12,691.39
Brian	Apr	$ 19,521.37
Brian	May	$ 16,579.38
Brian	Jun	$ 14,161.52
Chris	Jan	$ 2,792.18
Chris	Feb	$ 5,669.46
Chris	Mar	$ 4,909.24
Chris	Apr	$ 8,731.14
Chris	May	$ 11,747.29
Chris	Jun	$ 13,856.17

Wide format:

Salesperson	Jan	Feb	Mar	Apr	May	Jun
Abbie	$10,144.75	$29,008.52	$208,187.70	$21,502.13	$23,975.73	$20,172.20
Brian	$ 9,925.44	$ 9,183.93	$ 12,691.39	$19,521.37	$16,579.38	$14,161.52
Chris	$ 2,792.18	$ 5,669.46	$ 4,909.24	$ 8,731.14	$11,747.29	$13,856.17

FIGURE 7-9: A long dataset and a wide spreadsheet.

A *PivotTable* is a table that's derived from data that sits within a spreadsheet. The pivot allows for grouping, rearrangement, display, and summary of the raw data that's stored within the underlying spreadsheet.

The way that Excel is designed leads many users to intuitively prefer the wide format — which makes sense because it's a spreadsheet application. To counter this preference, however, Excel offers the PivotTable feature so that you can quickly convert between long and wide formats. You can also use PivotTables to quickly calculate subtotals and summary calculations on your newly formatted and rearranged data tables.

Creating PivotTables is easy: Just select all cells that comprise the table you want to analyze. Then click the PivotTable button on the Insert tab. This action opens the Create PivotTable dialog box, where you can define where you want Excel to construct the PivotTable. Click OK, and Excel automatically generates a PivotField Interface on the page you've specified. From this interface, you can specify the fields you want to include in the PivotTable and how you want them to be laid out.

The table shown in Figure 7-10 was constructed using the long-format sales performance data shown in Figure 7-9. It's an example of the simplest possible PivotTable that can be constructed, but even at that, it automatically calculates subtotals for each column and those subtotals automatically update when you make changes to the data. What's more, PivotTables come with *PivotCharts* — data plots that automatically change when you make changes to the PivotTable filters based on the criteria you're evaluating.

Total_Sales Salesperson	Month Jan	Feb	Mar	Apr	May	Jun	Grand Total
Abbie	$10,144.75	$29,008.52	$20,818.77	$21,502.13	$23,975.73	$20,172.20	$125,622.10
Brian	$9,925.44	$9,183.93	$12,691.39	$19,521.37	$16,579.38	$14,161.52	$82,063.03
Chris	$2,792.18	$5,669.46	$4,909.24	$8,731.14	$11,747.29	$13,856.17	$47,705.48
Grand Total	$22,862.37	$43,861.91	$38,419.40	$49,754.64	$52,302.40	$48,189.89	$255,390.61

FIGURE 7-10: Creating a wide data table from the long dataset via a PivotTable.

You can do a lot more sophisticated analytical work in Excel than just creating PivotTables, although they are handy. On the companion website to this book (https://businessgrowth.ai), I give you some basic training in how to use Excel and XLMiner to implement data science without needing to touch a single line of code.

Automating Excel tasks with macros

Macros are prescripted routines written in Visual Basic for Applications (VBA). You can use macros to decrease the amount of manual processing you need to do when working with data in Excel. For example, within Excel, macros can act as a set of functions and commands that you can use to automate a wide variety of tasks. If you want to save time (and hassle) by automating Excel tasks that you routinely repeat, use macros.

To access macros, first activate Excel's Developer tab from within the Options menu on the File tab. (In other words, after opening the Options menu, choose Customize Ribbon from your choices on the left and then click to select the Developer check box in the column on the right.) Using the Developer tab, you can record a macro, import one that was created by someone else, or code your own in VBA.

To illustrate macros in action, imagine that you have a column of values and you want to insert an empty cell between each one of the values, as shown in Figure 7-11. Excel has no easy, out-of-the-box way to make this insertion. Using Excel macros, however, you can ask Excel to record you while you step through the process one time, and then assign a key command to this recording to create the macro. After you create the macro, every time you need to repeat the same task in the future, just run the macro by pressing the key command, and the script then performs all required steps for you.

REMEMBER

Macros have an Absolute mode and a Relative mode. The Absolute mode refers to a macro's routine that runs absolutely the way you recorded it — all the way down to the spreadsheet cell positions in which the routine was recorded. Relative mode macros run the same routine you record but can be placed in whatever cell position you need within the spreadsheet.

TIP

When you record a macro, it records in Absolute mode by default. If you want it to record the macro in Relative mode instead, you need to select the Use Relative References option before recording the macro.

Before macro: After macro:

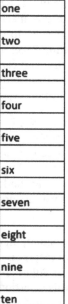

FIGURE 7-11: Using a macro to insert empty cells between values.

For a more formal definition of Absolute and Relative macros, consider this:

>> **Relative:** Every action and movement you make is recorded as relative to the cell that was selected when you began the recording. When you run the macro in the future, it will run in reference to the cell that's selected, acting as though that cell were the same cell you had initially selected when you recorded the macro.

>> **Absolute:** After you start recording the macro, every action and movement you make is repeated when you run the macro in the future, and those actions or movements aren't made in any relative reference to whatever cell was active when you started recording. The macro routine is repeated exactly as you recorded it.

In the preceding example, the macro was recorded in Relative mode. This enables the macro to be run continuously, anywhere, and on top of results from any preceding macros run. Because, in this scenario, the macro recorded only one iteration of the process, if it had been recorded in Absolute mode, every time it was run the macro would have kept adding a space between only the one and two values. In other words, it would not have operated on any cells other than the ones it was recorded on.

WARNING

Macro commands aren't entered into Excel's Undo stack. If you use a macro to change or delete data, you're stuck with that change.

Test your macros first and save your worksheets before using them so you can revert to the saved file if something goes wrong.

TIP

Excel power users often graduate to programming their own macros using VBA. Because VBA is a full-fledged programming language, the possibilities from pairing Excel with VBA are almost endless. Still, ask yourself this question: If you're going to invest time in learning a programming language, do you need to work within the confines of Excel's spreadsheet structure? If not, you may consider learning a scientific computing language, like R or Python. These open-source languages have a more user-friendly syntax and are much more flexible and powerful.

IN THIS CHAPTER

» **Laying out the basics of data visualization and storytelling**

» **Choosing the perfect data visualization type for the needs of your audience**

» **Picking the perfect design style**

» **Crafting clear and powerful visual messages with the right data graphic**

» **Adding context**

Chapter **8**

Telling Powerful Stories with Data

ny standard definition of data science will specify that its purpose is to help you extract meaning and value from raw data. Finding and deriving insights from raw data is at the crux of data science, but these insights mean nothing if you don't know how to communicate your findings to others. Data visualization and storytelling are excellent means by which you can visually communicate your data's meaning. To design effective data visualizations and stories, however, you must know and truly understand the target audience and the core purpose for which you're communicating with members of that audience. You must also understand the main types of data graphics that are available to you, as well as the significant benefits and drawbacks of each one. In this chapter, I present you with the core principles of data visualization and data storytelling design.

A *data visualization* is a visual representation that's designed for the purpose of conveying the meaning and significance of data and data insights. Because data visualizations are designed for a whole spectrum of different audiences, different purposes, and different skill levels, the first step to designing an effective data visualization is to *know your audience*. Audiences come in all shapes, forms, and sizes. You might design a data visualization for the young and edgy readers of *Wired* magazine or convey scientific findings to a research group. Your audience might consist of board members and organizational decision-makers or a local grassroots organization.

The one thing that's consistent across all audiences, however, is the process you should follow when creating your data visualization:

1. **Determine the type of data visualization you'll create, based on your audience and the purpose of your visualization.**

2. **Decide on a design style for your data visualization.**

3. **Choose which graphics make the most sense for your audience.**

4. **Test out different types of data graphics with the data, and then pick the ones that display the clearest and most obvious answers.**

5. **Arrange your data graphics within the data visualization.**

6. **Where appropriate, add context to enhance the meaning of the visualization.**

In this chapter, I walk you through all these steps in sequential order.

Data Visualizations: The Big Three

Every audience is composed of a unique class of consumers, each with unique data visualization needs, so you have to clarify for whom you're designing. Here are the types of data visualization and which audiences they're best for:

>> **Data storytelling:** Less-technical business decision-makers

>> **Data showcasing:** Data implementers, analysts, engineers, scientists, or statisticians

>> **Data art:** Idealists, dreamers, and social change-makers

I cover each of these types of data visualization in greater detail in the following sections.

Data storytelling for decision-makers

Sometimes, you have to design data visualizations for a less technical-minded audience, perhaps in order to help members of this audience make better-informed business decisions. The purpose of this type of visualization is to tell your audience the story behind the data. In data storytelling, the audience depends on you to make sense of the data behind the visualization and then turn useful insights into visual stories that they can easily understand.

With *data storytelling,* your goal should be to use data visualization, words, and presentation skills to create a narrative that tells the story — the *meaning,* in other words — of the data insights you seek to convey. With respect to the data visualization you use within a data story, you want it to be a clutter-free, highly focused visualization that enables your audience members to quickly extract meaning without having to make much effort. These visualizations are best delivered in the form of static images, but more adept decision-makers may prefer to have an interactive dashboard that they can use to do a bit of exploration and what-if modeling.

Data storytelling involves more than just data visualization design, though. You need to use words and presentation skills to communicate the data story as well. You'll want to use words sparingly within annotations on the data visualization itself. Maybe you present the data story with an accompanying slideshow, or maybe not — but you should present it with effective presentation skills.

Data showcasing for analysts

If you're designing for a crowd of data implementers or other logical, calculating analysts, you can create data visualizations that are rather open-ended. The purpose of this type of visualization is to help audience members visually explore the data and draw their own conclusions.

When using *data showcasing* techniques, your goal should be to display a lot of contextual information that supports audience members as they make their own interpretations. These visualizations should include more contextual data and less conclusive focus so that people can get in, analyze the data for themselves, and then draw their own conclusions. These visualizations are best delivered as static images or dynamic, interactive dashboards.

Designing data art for activists

You might design for an audience of idealists, dreamers, and change-makers. When designing for this particular audience, you want your data visualization to make a point! You can assume that typical audience members aren't overly analytical. What they lack in math skills, however, they more than compensate for in solid convictions.

These people look to your data visualization as a vehicle by which to make a statement. When designing for this audience, data art is the way to go. The main goal in using *data art* is to entertain, to provoke, to annoy, or to do whatever it takes to make a loud, clear, attention-demanding statement. Data art has little to no narrative and offers no room for viewers to form their own interpretations.

REMEMBER

Data scientists have an ethical responsibility to always represent data accurately. A data scientist should never distort the message of the data to fit what the audience wants to hear — not even for data art! Nontechnical audiences don't even recognize, let alone see, the possible issues. They rely on the data scientist to provide honest and accurate representations, thus amplifying the level of ethical responsibility that the data scientist must assume.

Designing to Meet the Needs of Your Target Audience

To make a functional data visualization, you must get to know your target audience and then design precisely for their needs. But to make every design decision with your target audience in mind, you need to take a few steps to make sure that you truly understand your data visualization's target consumers.

To gain the insights you need about your audience and your purpose, follow this process:

1. **Brainstorm.**

   Think about a specific member of your audience and make as many educated guesses as you can about that person's motivations.

Give this (imaginary) audience member a name and a few other identifying characteristics. I always imagine a 45-year-old divorced mother of two named Eve.

2. **Define the purpose of your visualization.**

   Narrow the purpose of the visualization by deciding exactly what action or outcome you want audience members to make as a result of the visualization.

3. **Choose a functional design.**

   Review the three main data visualization types (discussed earlier in this chapter) and decide which type can best help you achieve your intended outcome.

The following sections spell out this process in detail.

Step 1: Brainstorm (All about Eve)

To brainstorm properly, pull out a sheet of paper and picture an imaginary audience member — "Eve," for example. Let's practice together in creating a more functional and effective data visualization. You'd want to start by answering the more important questions you could ask about Eve in order to better understand her and, thus, better understand and design for your target audience.

Start by forming a picture of what Eve's average day looks like — what she does when she gets out of bed in the morning, what she does over her lunch hour, and what her workplace is like. Also consider how Eve will use your visualization. These things tell you a little bit about her *psychographics* (the psychological characteristics that drive her high-level needs and wants).

To form a more comprehensive view of who Eve is and how you can best meet her needs, you can pull from the following question bank:

>> Where does Eve work? What does she do for a living?

>> What kind of technical education or experience, if any, does she have?

>> How old is Eve? Is she married? Does she have children? What does she look like? Where does she live?

>> What social, political, cause-based, or professional issues are important to Eve? What does she think of herself?

>> What problems and issues does Eve have to deal with every day?

>> How does your data visualization help solve Eve's work problems or her family problems? How does it improve her self-esteem?

>> Through what avenue will you present the visualization to Eve (for example, over the internet or in a staff meeting)?

>> What does Eve need to be able to do with your data visualization?

Because we're doing this together, I'll answer these questions for you by telling you that Eve is the manager of the zoning department in Irvine County. She is 45 years old and a divorced mother of two children who are about to start college. She is deeply interested in local politics and eventually wants to be on the county's board of commissioners. To achieve that position, she has to get some major "oomph" on her county management résumé. Eve derives most of her feelings of self-worth from her job and her keen ability to make good management decisions for her department.

Until now, Eve has been forced to manage her department according to her gut-level intuition, backed by a few disparate business systems reports. She isn't extraordinarily analytical, but she knows enough to understand what she sees. The problem is that Eve lacks the visualization tools she needs in order to display all the relevant data she should consider. She has neither the time nor the skill to code something herself. Eve is excited that you'll attend next Monday's staff meeting to present data insights you've discovered that she hopes will enable her to make more effective data-driven management decisions.

Step 2: Define the purpose

After you brainstorm about the typical audience member (see the preceding section), you can much more easily pinpoint exactly what you're trying to achieve with your data visualization. Are you trying to get consumers to feel a certain way about themselves or the world around them? Are you trying to make a statement? Are you seeking to influence organizational decision-makers to make good business decisions? Or do you simply want to lay all the data out there, for all viewers to make sense of, and deduce from it what they will?

Returning to the hypothetical Eve: What decisions or processes are you trying to help her achieve? Well, you'd first need to make sense of her data and uncover relevant data insights. Then you'd need to present those data insights to her in a way that she can clearly understand and use for improved decision-making. So, looking at the data — what do you see that's happening within the inner mechanics of Eve's department? After you've discovered some clear trends and predictions, it's time to use data visualization skills to guide Eve into making the most prudent and effective management choices.

Step 3: Choose the most functional visualization type for your purpose

Keep in mind that you have three main types of visualization from which to choose: data storytelling, data art, and data showcasing. Remember that, if you're designing for organizational decision-makers, you'll most likely use data storytelling to directly tell your audience what their data means with respect to their line of business. If you're designing for a social justice organization or a political campaign, data art can best make a dramatic and effective statement with your data. Lastly, if you're designing for analysts, engineers, scientists, or statisticians, stick with data showcasing so that these analytical types have plenty of room to figure things out on their own.

Back to Eve — because she's not extraordinarily analytical and because she's depending on you to help her make excellent data-driven decisions, you need to employ *data storytelling* techniques. Create either a static or interactive data visualization with some, but not too much, context. The visual elements of the design should tell a clear story about her business unit, such that Eve doesn't have to work through tons of complexity to get the point of what you're trying to tell her about her department.

TIP

My best practices for effective dashboard design are available to you over on https://businessgrowth.ai.

Picking the Most Appropriate Design Style

If you're the analytical type, you might say that the only purpose of a data visualization is to convey numbers and facts via charts and graphs — no beauty or design is needed. But if you're a more artistic-minded person, you may insist that you have to *feel* something in order to truly understand it. Truth be told, a good data visualization is neither artless and dry nor completely abstract in its artistry. Instead, its beauty and design lie somewhere on the spectrum between these two extremes.

To choose the most appropriate design style, you must first consider your audience (discussed earlier in this chapter) and then decide how you want them to respond to your visualization. If you're looking to entice the audience into taking a deeper, more analytical dive into the visualization, employ a design style that induces a calculating and exacting response in its viewers. But if you want your data visualization to fuel your audience's passion, use an emotionally compelling design style instead.

Inducing a calculating, exacting response

If you're designing a data visualization for corporate types, engineers, scientists, or organizational decision-makers, keep the design simple and sleek, using the data showcasing or data storytelling visualization. To induce a logical, calculating feel in your audience, include a lot of bar charts, scatterplots, and line charts. Color choices here should be rather traditional and conservative. The look and feel should scream "corporate chic" (see Figure 8-1). Visualizations of this style are meant to quickly and clearly communicate what's happening in the data — direct, concise, and to the point. The best data visualizations of this style convey an elegant look and feel.

TIP

If you're looking for guidance on the best web applications for data visualization and storytelling, be sure to check out my *Web-Based Data Visualization Design Tools: Top 10 Guide* at https://businessgrowth.ai.

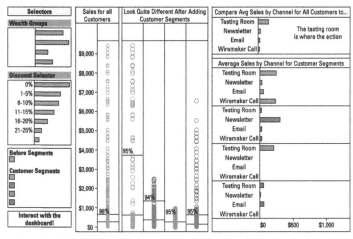

FIGURE 8-1: This design style conveys a calculating and exacting feel.

Eliciting a strong emotional response

If you're designing a data visualization to influence or persuade people, incorporate design artistry that invokes an emotional response in your target audience. These visualizations usually fall under the data art category, but an extremely creative data storytelling piece can also inspire this sort of strong emotional response. Emotionally provocative data visualizations often support the stance of one side of a social, political, or environmental issue. These data visualizations include fluid, artistic design elements that flow and meander, as shown in Figure 8-2. Additionally, rich, dramatic color choices can influence the emotions of the viewer. This style of data visualization leaves a lot of room for artistic creativity and experimentation.

TIP

Keep artistic elements relevant — and recognize when they're likely to detract from the impression you want to make, particularly when you're designing for analytical types.

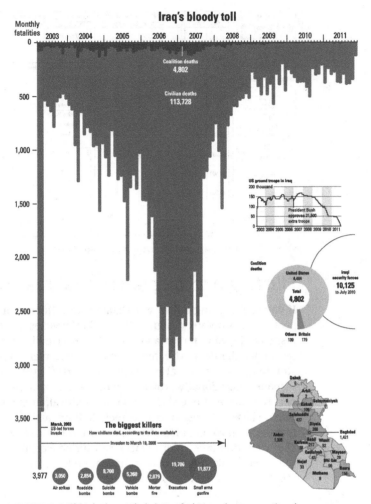

FIGURE 8-2: This design style is intended to evoke an emotional response.

Selecting the Appropriate Data Graphic Type

Your choice of data graphic type can make or break a data visualization. In case it's unclear, a *data graphic* is the graphical element that depicts your data insight in visual format (see Figure 8-3). Most data visualizations have more than one data graphic within them.

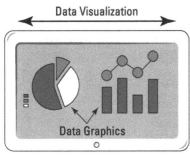

FIGURE 8-3: Data visualization versus data graphics.

Because you probably need to represent many different facets of your data, you can mix and match among the different graphical classes and types. Even among the same class, certain graphic types perform better than others; therefore, it's a good idea to create several different mockups to see which graphic type conveys the clearest and most obvious message.

WARNING

This book introduces only the most commonly used graphic types (among hundreds that are available). Don't wander too far off the beaten path. The further you stray from familiar graphics, the harder it becomes for people to understand the information you're trying to convey.

REMEMBER

Pick the graphic type that most dramatically displays the data trends you're seeking to reveal. (Figure 8-4 lists some general guidelines.) You can display the same data trend in many ways, but some methods deliver a visual message more effectively than others. The point is to deliver a clear, comprehensive visual message to your audience so people can use the visualization to help them make sense of the data presented.

Among the most useful types of data graphics are standard chart graphics, comparative graphics, statistical plots, topology structures, and spatial plots and maps. The next few sections take a look at each of these types.

Data Graphic Types	Visualization Element	Data Storytelling audience: less-technical business decision-makers	Data Showcasing audience: data implementers, analysts, engineers, scientists, or statisticians	Data Art audience: idealists, dreamers, and social change-makers
Standard Chart Graphics	Bar Chart	☑	☑	☑
	Line Chart	☑	☑	☑
	Pie Chart	☑	☐	☑
Comparative Graphics	Bubble Plots	☑	☑	☑
	Packed Circle Diagrams	☐	☑	☐
	Gantt Charts	☑	☑	☐
	Stacked Charts	☐	☑	☐
	Tree Maps	☐	☑	☐
	Word Clouds	☑	☑	☑
Statistical Plots	Histogram	☐	☑	☐
	Scatter Plot	☐	☑	☐
	Scatter Plot Matrix	☐	☑	☐
Topology Structures	Linear Topology Structures	☑	☑	☑
	Graph Models	☐	☑	☑
	Tree Network Topology	☑	☑	☑
Spatial Plots and Maps	Cloropleth	☑	☑	☑
	Point	☑	☑	☑
	Raser Surface	☐	☑	☐
Contextual Elements	Contextual Data Graphics	☐	☑	☑
	Annotations	☑	☑	☐
	Trend Lines	☑	☑	☑
	Single-Value Alerts	☑	☑	☐
	Target Trend Lines	☑	☑	☐
	Predictive Benchmarks	☑	☑	☐

FIGURE 8-4: Types of data graphics, broken down by audience and data visualization type.

Standard chart graphics

When making data visualizations for an audience of nonanalytical people, stick to standard chart graphics. The more complex your graphics, the harder it is for nonanalytical people to understand them. And not all standard chart types are boring. You have quite a variety to choose from:

>> **Area charts** (see Figure 8-5) are a fun-yet-simple way to visually compare and contrast attribute values. You can use this type of chart to effectively tell a visual story when you've chosen data storytelling and data showcasing. Not all area charts are 3-D, like the one shown in Figure 8-5, but they all represent numerical values by the proportion of area those values consume visually on the chart.

Population from 1957 to 2007 [Gapminder]

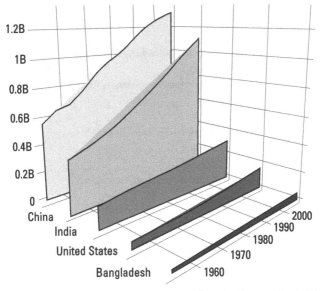

Source: Lynda . com, Python for DS

FIGURE 8-5: An area chart in three dimensions.

>> **Bar charts** (see Figure 8-6) are a simple way to visually compare and contrast values of parameters in the same category. Bar charts are best for data storytelling and data showcasing.

>> **Line charts** (see Figure 8-7) most commonly show changes in time series data, but they can also plot relationships between two, or even three, parameters. Line charts are so versatile that you can use them in all data visualization design types.

>> **Pie charts** (see Figure 8-8), which are among the most commonly used, provide a simple way to compare values of parameters in the same category. Their simplicity, however, can be a double-edged sword; deeply analytical people tend to scoff at them, precisely because they seem so simple, so you may want to consider omitting them from data-showcasing visualizations.

CHAPTER 8 **Telling Powerful Stories with Data** 155

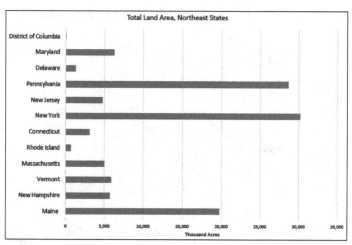

FIGURE 8-6: A bar chart showing the area of U.S. states by their acreage, in thousand acres.

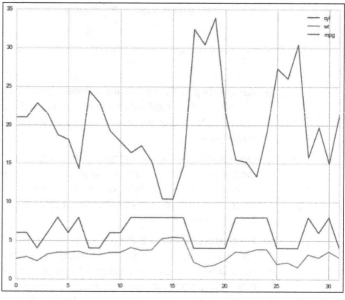

Source: Lynda.com, Python for DS

FIGURE 8-7: A line chart.

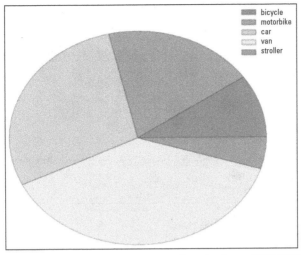

Source: Lynda . com, Python for DS

FIGURE 8-8: A pie chart.

Comparative graphics

A *comparative graphic* displays the relative value of multiple parameters in a shared category or the relatedness of parameters within multiple shared categories. The core difference between comparative graphics and standard graphics is that comparative graphics offer you a way to simultaneously compare more than one parameter and category. Standard graphics, on the other hand, provide a way to view and compare only the difference between one parameter of any single category. Comparative graphics are geared toward an audience that's at least slightly analytical, so you can easily use these graphics in either data storytelling or data showcasing. Visually speaking, comparative graphics are more complex than standard graphics.

This list shows a few different types of popular comparative graphics:

>> **Bubble plots** (see Figure 8-9) use bubble size and color to demonstrate the relationship between three parameters of the same category.

>> **Packed circle diagrams** (see Figure 8-10) use both circle size and clustering to visualize the relationships between categories, parameters, and relative parameter values.

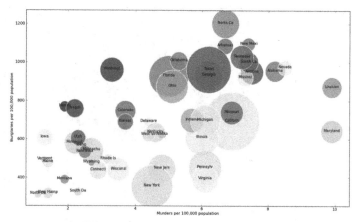

FIGURE 8-9: A bubble chart.

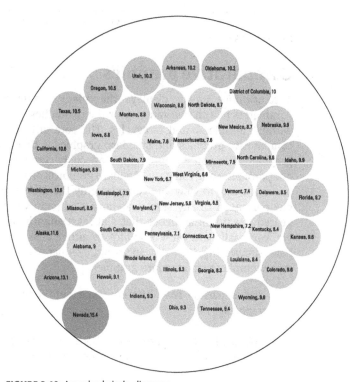

FIGURE 8-10: A packed circle diagram.

TIP

>> **Gantt charts** (see Figure 8-11) are bar charts that use horizontal bars to visualize scheduling requirements for project management purposes. This type of chart is useful when you're developing a plan for project delivery. It's also helpful in determining the sequence in which tasks must be completed in order to meet delivery timelines.

Choose Gantt charts for project management and scheduling.

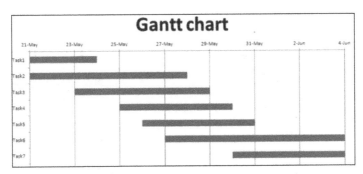

FIGURE 8-11: A Gantt chart.

>> **Stacked charts** (see Figure 8-12) are used to compare multiple attributes of parameters in the same category. To ensure that it doesn't become difficult to make a visual comparison, resist the urge to include too many parameters.

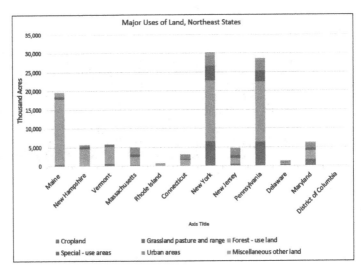

FIGURE 8-12: A stacked chart.

>> **Tree maps** (see Figure 8-13) aggregate parameters of like categories and then use area to show the relative size of each category compared to the whole.

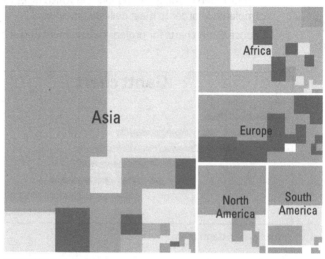

FIGURE 8-13: A tree map.

>> **Word clouds** (see Figure 8-14) use size and color to show the relative difference in frequency of words used in a body of text. Colors are generally employed to indicate classifications of words by usage type.

FIGURE 8-14: A simple word cloud.

Statistical plots

Statistical plots, which show the results of statistical analyses, are usually useful only to a deeply analytical audience (and aren't useful for making data art). Here are your statistical plot choices:

TIP

>> **Histograms** (shown in Figure 8-15) are diagrams that plot a variable's frequency and distribution as rectangles on a chart. A histogram can help you quickly get a handle on the distribution and frequency of data in a dataset.

Get comfortable with histograms. You'll see a lot of them in the course of making statistical analyses.

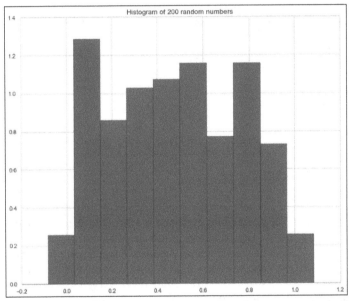

Source: Lynda.com, Python for DS

FIGURE 8-15: A histogram.

>> **Scatterplots** (see Figure 8-16) plot data points according to their *x*- and *y*-values in order to visually reveal any significant patterns. A scatterplot is a terrific way to quickly uncover significant trends and outliers in a dataset. If you use data storytelling or data showcasing, start by generating a quick

scatterplot to get a feel for areas in the dataset that may be interesting — areas that can potentially uncover significant relationships or yield persuasive stories.

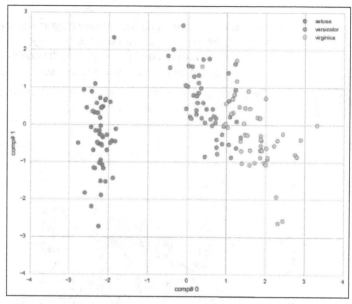

Source: Lynda.com, Python for DS

FIGURE 8-16: A scatterplot.

>> **Scatterplot matrixes** (see Figure 8-17) place a number of related scatterplots in a visual series that shows correlations between multiple variables. A scatterplot matrix is a good choice when you want to explore the relationships between several variables. Discovering and verifying relationships between variables can help you to identify clusters among variables and identify oddball outliers in your dataset.

Topology structures

Topology is the practice of using geometric structures to describe and model the relationships and connectedness between entities and variables in a dataset. You need to understand basic topology structures so you can accurately structure your visual display to match the fundamental underlying structure of the concepts you're representing.

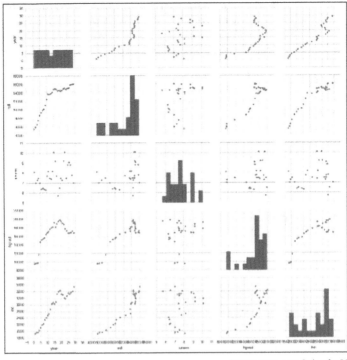

Source: Lynda . com, Python for DS

FIGURE 8-17: A scatterplot matrix.

The following list describes a series of topological structures that are popular in data science:

>> **Linear topological structures** (see Figure 8-18) represent a pure one-to-one relationship. They're often used in data visualizations that depict time series flow patterns. Any process that can occur only by way of a sequential series of dependent events is linear, and you can effectively represent it by using this underlying topological structure.

FIGURE 8-18: A linear topology.

>> **Graph models** (see Figure 8-19) underlie group communication networks and traffic flow patterns. You can use graph topology to represent many-to-many relationships, like those that form the basis of social media platforms.

REMEMBER

In a *many-to-many* relationship structure, each variable or entity has more than one link to the other variables or entities in that same dataset.

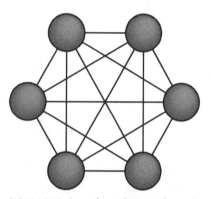

FIGURE 8-19: A graph mesh network topology.

>> **Tree network topologies** (see Figure 8-20) represent a *hierarchical* classification, where a network is distributed in top-down order — nodes act as receivers and distributors of connections, and lines represent the connections between nodes. End nodes act only as receivers and not as distributors. Hierarchical classification underlies clustering and machine learning methodologies in data science. Tree network structures can represent one-to-many relationships, such as the ones that underlie a family tree or a taxonomy structure.

Spatial plots and maps

Spatial plots and maps are two different ways of visualizing spatial data. A *map* is just a plain figure that represents the location, shape, and size of features on the face of the earth. A *spatial plot*, which is visually more complex than a map, shows the values for — and location distribution of — a spatial feature's attributes.

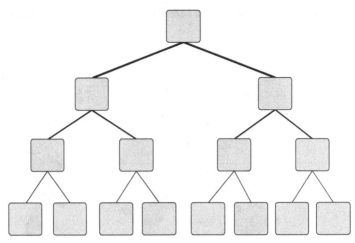

FIGURE 8-20: A hierarchical tree topology.

Here are a few types of spatial plots and maps that are commonly used in data visualization:

» **Cloropleth:** Despite its fancy name, a Cloropleth map (see Figure 8-21) is really just spatial data plotted out according to area boundary polygons rather than by point, line, or raster coverage. On the map in Figure 8-21, each state boundary represents an *area boundary* polygon. The color and shade of the area within each boundary represents the relative value of the attribute for that state — where red areas have a higher attribute value and blue areas have a smaller attribute value.

» **Point:** Composed of spatial data that is plotted out according to specific point locations, a point map (see Figure 8-22) presents data in a graphical point form rather than in a polygon, line, or raster surface format.

» **Raster surface:** A raster surface map (see Figure 8-23) can be anything from a satellite image map to a surface coverage with values that have been interpolated from underlying spatial data points.

TIP

For a training on how to make maps from data using QGIS, an open-source geographic information system (GIS) application, visit https://businessgrowth.ai.

Average SATm Score for Graduating High School Student

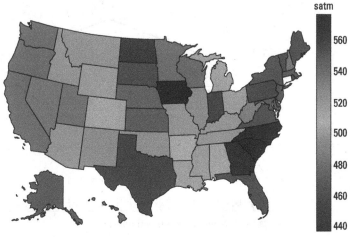

satm

560
540
520
500
480
460
440

Source: Lynda.com, Python for DS

FIGURE 8-21: A Cloropleth map.

Region 3 - Active, Decreed Wells

N

FIGURE 8-22: A point map.

REMEMBER

Whether you're a data visualization designer or a consumer, be aware of some common pitfalls in data visualization. Simply put, a data visualization can be misleading if it isn't constructed correctly. Common problems include pie charts that don't add up to

100 percent, bar charts with a scale that starts in a strange place, and multicolumn bar charts with vertical axes that don't match.

Kriged Raster Surface Overlay

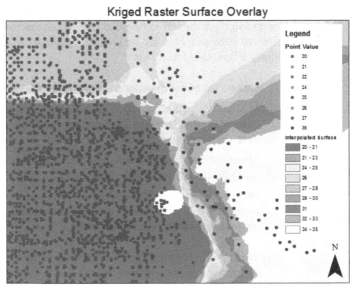

FIGURE 8-23: A raster surface map.

Testing Data Graphics

Your data visualizations must convey clear and powerful visual messages. To make that happen, you have to test various data graphics and select only the most effective ones to include in the final data visualization. For example, the two data graphics shown in Figure 8-24 represent exactly the same statistic.

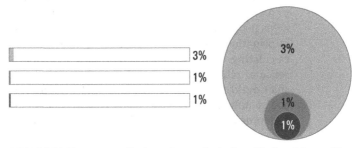

FIGURE 8-24: Here you see the importance of selecting effective data graphics.

Notice how the data graphic on the right does a much better job of visually emphasizing the difference in numeric values? You should always test different data graphics, to make sure that you use the one that most clearly and effectively displays your data. The graphic on the left is *not* effective. To choose only the most effective data graphics for inclusion in your data visualization, simply follow these four steps:

1. **Make a list of the questions that your data is meant to answer.**

2. **Determine the data visualization type: data storytelling, data showcasing, or data art.**

3. **Select options from among appropriate data graphic types for that type of data visualization.**

4. **Test those data graphics with your data — see for yourself which graphic type displays the most clear and obvious answers to your questions.**

TIP

After testing different data graphics and deciding what you want to use, arrange those graphics within your data visualization. You can do that using either Python or R or a spreadsheet (see Chapter 6). Alternatively, to create your data visualization using an online data visualization design tool, you may find my guide helpful: *Web-Based Data Visualization Design Tools — Top 10*. You can find it at https://businessgrowth.ai.

Adding Context

After you know exactly which data graphics you'll use, you need to decide whether and how you'll create the necessary context to add more meaning to the data visualization. Adding context helps people understand the value and relative significance of the information your data visualization conveys. Adding context to calculating, exacting data visualization styles helps to create a sense of relative perspective, but in pure data art you may consider omitting additional context. That's because, with data art, you're only trying to make a single point and you don't want to add information that would distract from that point.

Creating context with data

In data showcasing, you should include relevant contextual data for the key metrics shown in your data visualization — in a situation where you're creating a data visualization that describes conversion rates for e-commerce sales, for example. The key metric would be represented by the percentage of users who convert to customers by making a purchase. Contextual data that's relevant to this metric may include shopping cart abandonment rates, average number of sessions before a user makes a purchase, average number of pages visited before making a purchase, or specific pages that are visited before a customer decides to convert. This sort of contextual information helps viewers understand the why and how behind sales conversions.

REMEMBER

Adding contextual data tends to decentralize the focus of a data visualization, so add this data only in visualizations that are intended for an analytical audience. These folks are in a better position to assimilate the extra information and use it to draw their own conclusions; with other types of audiences, context is only a distraction.

Creating context with annotations

Sometimes, you can more appropriately create context by including annotations that provide a header and a small description of the context of the data that's shown (see Figure 8-25). This method of creating context is most appropriate for data storytelling or data showcasing. Good annotation is helpful to both analytical and nonanalytical audiences alike.

Creating context with graphical elements

Another effective way to create context in a data visualization is to include graphical elements that convey the relative significance of the data. Such graphical elements include moving average trend lines, single-value alerts, target trend lines (as shown in Figure 8-26), and predictive benchmarks.

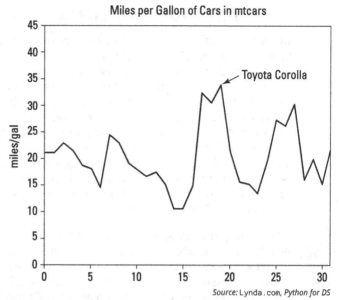

Source: Lynda.com, *Python for DS*

FIGURE 8-25: Using annotation to create context.

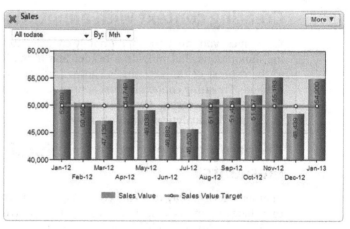

FIGURE 8-26: Using graphical elements to create context.

Chapter **9**

Ten Free or Low-Cost Data Science Libraries and Platforms

Because data collection, analysis, and visualization comprise the crux of the data scientist's toolkit, it should come as no surprise that you can use quite a few free libraries, tools, and platforms to carry out these tasks with greater ease. In this chapter, I present ten free or low-cost applications you can use to complete data science tasks.

TIP

For a little extra guidance on how to use the Python libraries discussed in this chapter, check out my LinkedIn Learning courses, available at www.linkedin.com/learning/instructors/lillian-pierson-p-e.

Scraping the Web with Beautiful Soup

Beautiful Soup (https://beautiful-soup-4.readthedocs.io/en/latest) is a popular Python library that's built to support most web-scraping requirements. If you need to extract data from websites, this is the library for you. It completely simplifies the process of navigating, searching, and modifying web page content. Beautiful Soup is especially useful for tasks like collecting large datasets from the web, gathering information for research, or automating repetitive web data collection.

REMEMBER

In web scraping, you set up automated programs and then let those programs scour the web for the data you need.

Wrangling Data with pandas

Python's pandas library (https://pandas.pydata.org) is a free option that you can use to manipulate, clean, and analyze structured data. Whether you're working with comma-separated values (CSV) files, Microsoft Excel files, or data from Structured Query Language (SQL) databases, pandas provides an intuitive way to reshape, filter, and aggregate your data. With its large community and extensive documentation, pandas is an excellent option for any data-wrangling tasks you may find yourself up against.

Visualizing Data with Looker Studio

Looker Studio (https://lookerstudio.google.com), formerly known as Google Data Studio, has evolved into a powerful data analytics platform that enables users to analyze data from a wide variety of sources, including databases, data warehouses, and third-party applications — not just Google Analytics. It's a free, cloud-based data visualization and business intelligence tool that you can use to turn raw data into insightful, shareable reports and dashboards. If you're looking to make data-driven decisions with clear and interactive reports, be sure to explore what Looker Studio can do for you.

Machine Learning with scikit-learn

Machine learning is the class of artificial intelligence (AI) that's dedicated to developing and applying algorithms to data so that the algorithms can automatically learn and detect patterns in large datasets. One of the most important libraries for machine learning is scikit-learn (https://scikit-learn.org), a user-friendly and versatile Python library that simplifies the process of building, training, and evaluating machine learning models. It's widely used for traditional machine learning tasks like classification, regression, clustering, and dimension reduction.

Creating Interactive Dashboards with Streamlit

Streamlit (`https://streamlit.io`) is a powerful and easy-to-use Python library for building interactive web applications and data dashboards. You can use it to quickly transform Python scripts into web-based applications, even if you don't have web development expertise. Streamlit's simplicity and flexibility have made it an increasingly popular choice for creating data science prototypes, dashboards, and even machine learning model demonstrations.

Doing Geospatial Data Visualization with Kepler.gl

Kepler.gl (`https://kepler.gl`) is an open-source, high-performance tool that was developed by Uber for visualizing large-scale geospatial data. It makes it easy to explore, analyze, and present data within a geographical context. The tool is especially good at processing and displaying large datasets. It provides both flexibility and performance for working with spatial data.

Making Charts with Tableau Public

Tableau Public (`www.tableausoftware.com/public`), a free desktop application, aims to be a complete package for chart making. As part of the freeware limitation, the application doesn't let you save files locally to your computer. All your work must be uploaded to Tableau Public's cloud server, unless you purchase the software.

Tableau Public creates three levels of document: the worksheet, the dashboard, and the story. In the worksheet, you can create individual charts from data you've imported from Access, Excel, or a CSV file. You can then use Tableau Public to easily do things such as choose between different data graphic types or drag columns to different axes or subgroups.

Doing Web-Based Data Visualization with RAWGraphs

You can use RAWGraphs (www.rawgraphs.io), a unique and unusual web application, to make artistic and creative visualizations from your dataset. The RAWGraphs layout has a simple drag-and-drop interface that you can use to make unique and interesting data visualizations with just a few clicks of the mouse. If you want to get funky and cool with your data visualization but you lack the time or money it takes to learn how to code this sort of thing for yourself, RAWGraphs is the perfect data visualization alternative.

Making Cool Infographics with Infogram

You can use the online tool Infogram (https://infogram.com) to make aesthetically appealing, *vertically stacked card infographics* (visualizations that are composed of a series of cards, stacked vertically on top of one another, each with its own set of data graphics). Infogram offers a variety of trendy color schemes, design schemes, and chart types. With Infogram, you can import your own images to make an infographic that's much more personalized. Infogram also provides you with sharing capabilities so you can spread an infographic quickly and easily across social channels or via private email. The freemium plan is robust enough to supply all your more basic infographic-making needs.

Making Cool Infographics with Canva

Canva (www.canva.com) is a versatile tool that you can use to design professional infographics, even if you don't have advanced design skills. Canva's intuitive interface allows users to easily create infographics by dragging and dropping elements like text, images, and charts. No coding or design experience is required.

Index

L

labeled data, 81–82
labeled datasets, 80
latent variables, 49
lazy machine learning, 89
learning, 68
learning styles, 31–32
left join, 128
`len` function, 100
libraries and platforms
  about, 171
  Beautiful Soup, 171–172
  Canva, 174
  Infogram, 174
  Kepler.gl, 173
  Looker Studio, 172
  Pandas library, 172
  Python, 107–113
  RAWGraphs, 174
  scikit-learn, 172–173
  Streamlit, 173
  Tableau Public, 173–174
line charts, 155, 156
linear algebra, reducing data dimensionality with, 48–54
linear regression, 57–59
linear topological structures, 163
LinkedIn Learning, 96, 171
lists, in Python, 99, 100
local maximum density, 73
local minimum density, 73
`login_ftp` method, 106
logistic regression, 59
long, as a number type, 99
Looker, 25
Looker Studio, 172
loops, in Python, 101–103
low value, of data, 16
low-code, 117
low-density regions, 73

M

machine learning
  about, 19, 29–30, 68
  learning styles, 31–32
  processes of, 30
  terminology for, 30–31
  uses for, 32–37
machine learning engineers
  about, 20
  data science for, 14
  role of, 21–22
machine learning repository, 44
macros, automating Excel tasks with in Microsoft Excel, 139–141
Make, 116
Manhattan metric, 71, 76
many-to-many relationship structure, 164
MapReduce, 27, 37
marketing data scientists, data science for, 13
marketing strategy, 8
mathematical modeling, applying to data science tasks, 11
Matplotlib library, 97, 111–113
matrices, compressing sparse, 49
`MAX( )` function, 127, 130
MCDM (multiple criteria decision-making). *See* multiple criteria decision-making (MCDM)
mean function, 109
meaning, 146
methods, 105. *See also specific methods*
metric features, 52
Microsoft Access, 117
Microsoft Azure, 23, 24, 116
Microsoft Azure AI, 28
Microsoft Excel
  about, 118, 131–132

automating tasks with macros, 139–141
charting in, 135–137
filtering in, 132–134
getting to know data using, 132–137
reformatting using PivotTables, 137–138
summarizing using PivotTables, 137–138
using conditional formatting, 134–135
Microsoft Power Platform, 117
Microsoft SQL Server, 120
`MIN( )` function, 127, 130
Minkowski distance metric, 71
MLlib module (Apache Spark), 37
model overfitting, 33, 83–84
model overgeneralization, 83–84
modeling
  decisions with multiple criteria decision-making, 54–57
  univariate time series data, 65–66
MongoDB, 26, 36
moving average techniques, 65
multicollinearity, 60
multidimensional datasets, 48
multi-label learning, 91
MultinomialNB, 44
multiple criteria decision-making (MCDM)
  about, 54–55
  fuzzy, 57
  traditional, 55–56
multiple dependencies, 125
multiple linear regression, 58
multivariate analysis, detecting outliers with, 62–63
multivariate normality (MVN), 53
mutually exclusive, 43
MySQL, 120

N

Naïve Bayes
  conditional probability with, 44–45
  selecting algorithms for, 33
n-dimensional arrays, 107–108
n-dimensional plot, 71
nearest neighbor analysis
  about, 84–85
  algorithms for, 92–94
  average, 86–88
neural network, selecting algorithms for, 34–35
no-code, 117
noise, 41, 90
noisy data, 81
noncore samples, 77
nonglobular, 77
nonredundancy of columns, 125
nonstationary processes, 64–65
normal brackets, 101
normal distributions, 43
normalized data, 68
normalized databases, 124–127
NoSQL databases, 26
number of centroids, 72
numbers, in Python, 98, 99
numeric datasets, 71
numerical data type, 11, 124
NumPy library, 107–110

O

observation, 30
Open to Work, 96
OpenAI, 116
open-source geographic information system (GIS) (QGIS), 165
Oracle, 120
ordinal features, 53
ordinal variables, 43

ordinary least squares (OLS), 60
outer join, 128
outliers
  about, 60–61
  analyzing extreme values, 60–61
  collective, 77
  detecting, 60–63
overgeneralization, 83–84

P

packed circle diagrams, 157, 158
Pandas library, 111, 172
parentheses, 101
partitional algorithms, 69
PCA (principal component analysis), 48, 53–54, 63
Pearson's *r*, calculating correlation with, 45–46
Pentaho, 25
perceptron, 34
pie charts, 155, 157
Pierson, Lillian (author), contact information for, 4
PivotTables, reformatting and summarizing with, 137–138
platforms. *See* libraries and platforms
plot function, 112
.ply file format, 10
point map, 165, 166
point outliers, 61
population, 41
PostgreSQL, 17, 120
Power BI, 25
predictant, 57
predictive analytics, 54
predictive applications, containerizing within Kubernetes, 24
prescriptive analytics, 54
primary key, 120–123, 125
principal component analysis (PCA), 48, 53–54, 63

principal components, 53
print function, 99, 103
probability, 40–42
probability distributions, 42–43
processing, 22–27
purpose, designing, 148–149
pyplot function, 112
Python
  about, 37
  classes, 104–106
  in data science strategy, 95–96
  data types, 98–101
  enabling NumPy in, 108
  functions, 103–104
  libraries, 107–113
  loops in, 101–103
  using for data science, 96–113
Python for Data Science Essential Training courses, 2
PyTorch, 28

Q

QGIS (open-source geographic information system (GIS)), 165
Qlik, 25
quantifying correlation, 45–48
quantitative data, 11
query, 127
querying data, 9–11

R

R
  about, 37
  cluster package, 74
  hclust package, 77
random forest algorithms, categorizing data with, 79–80
random variable, 42

About the Author

Lillian Pierson, PE, is the founder and fractional CMO at Data-Mania, as well as a globally recognized growth leader in technology. To date, she has helped educate approximately 2 million professionals on topics related to AI, growth, data strategy, and data science.

She is the author of dozens of data-intensive books and courses, in deep partnership with both John Wiley & Sons and LinkedIn Learning, among others. Lillian has supported a wide variety of organizations globally, from the United Nations and *National Geographic* to Ericsson and Saudi Aramco and everything in between.

A licensed professional engineer in good standing, Lillian has been both a technical and marketing consultant since 2007 and a growth adviser since 2018.

Dedication

To Vitaly, Ariana, and Stasik. I love you all so much — you make my world go 'round.

Author's Acknowledgments

I extend a huge thanks to all the people who've helped me produce this book. Thanks so much to Chris Levesque, for your technical edits. Also, I extend a huge thanks to Lindsay Berg, Elizabeth Kuball, and the rest of the editorial and production staff at Wiley.

Publisher's Acknowledgments

Executive Editor: Lindsay Berg

Editor: Elizabeth Kuball

Production Editor: Saikarthick Kumarasamy

Cover Design and Image: Wiley